Foreword

I was introduced to Amber Miller, like many others in our community, through her articles in *The Bargain Hunter*. What a joy it was to discover someone who, like me, had so clearly experienced the joy and freedom of walking into the warm sunlight of the pure gospel, after being stuck so long in the shade of performance-based Christianity.

Reading through these articles once again in preparation for writing this foreword, I was struck by how her message of God's unhindered favor toward us continues to resonate so powerfully. I love the way Amber always seems ready and able to hear from God through the experiences of everyday life. There, she repeatedly discovers new facets of God's goodness and faithfully proclaims, through her writing, just how unbelievably good He is. Amber's gospel is bold and unashamed, yet she writes simply, with the humility befitting someone who has drunk deeply from the well of God's astounding love. The fruit of such love is so readily apparent in her and her family, as they live their lives honestly under the tender gaze of their Heavenly Daddy.

I am proud to call Amber and her family my friends and believe that her writings, carefully assembled here, will bless, strengthen, and encourage anyone who reads them.

—Brad Olsen
Lead Pastor
Berlin Christian Fellowship Church
Berlin, Ohio

Introduction

As you read these words, a dream of mine has been achieved. It is only one of the many dreams God has placed in my heart. It is a great feeling to see a dream come to fruition. And it is all because of God.

Almost four years ago, God started encouraging me to dream big. He showed me that He had a bigger plan for my life than what I was living. I wasn't living a sinful life; I just wasn't living out the plan that God had for me. I knew that but had two issues with it. The first issue I had was not knowing exactly what God had in mind for me to do. I would constantly ask, "Okay, God, what do You have for me? Is this it? Get up, go to work and be stressed, come home stressed while trying to take care of my family, and then go to sleep. Get up and repeat the process. Isn't there more to life than this? I want to enjoy life, but I also want to impact people. I want to make a difference."

As I learned more and more about the goodness of God and that He actually did have great plans for my life, I knew that something had to change. Then I heard a series of messages from a Bible teacher on how to *find, follow,* and *fulfill* God's will. That was exactly what I needed. I *knew* God had put this unrest in my heart because He didn't want me to be satisfied with living short of the plans He had for my life. Now He had put a new passion in my heart, a desire to live out the incredible plans He had for me. I didn't have everything figured out (and still don't), but I knew He had put a burning desire in my heart to share the gospel with others. When I was able to share with others, this passion arose out of my heart so strongly that I just knew that I knew this was what God had for me. I've never been high on drugs, but what I experienced after being able to share with others was a spiritual high.

My second issue was that my life was safe. I was doing the same thing I had been doing for the past ten years, and although I wasn't necessarily happy with it, moving out of my comfort zone made me a little nervous. I am a very routine-oriented person. I don't do crazy things. I mean, quitting my job after I had earned my college degree would be just a little crazy, wouldn't it? And leaving the comfort of two incomes to go down to one income, well that made me *very* nervous. Growing up the daughter of a banker, I was taught to manage my money wisely and stay out of debt. And we had achieved that. I took comfort in having more than enough each month to meet our needs. But I started believing that if God called me to something else, He would provide. He wasn't going to call me and then just leave me hanging. He has proved to be so faithful.

Healing was a big part of what I had been learning and sharing with people, though few received it. Because of some of the devastation I had gone through in my own family as a result of sickness, I wanted to tell others that God wanted them well and had already provided healing through the body of Jesus. So I thought maybe God had a healing ministry in store for me. Like I said, I didn't know all the details, but I knew it involved me, in some way, sharing the goodness of God with others.

Writing was another thing that God put on my heart. I enjoyed writing as a teenager, but I hadn't done it in years. I didn't think I was gifted; I just enjoyed doing it. I actually despised it in college because we were forced to write papers and there was so much formality tied to it. I thought maybe

God put in my heart to start writing children's books. No offense intended, but quite a few children's books leave a lot to be desired. Maybe that was what God had for me also? I just didn't know, but I knew that *nothing* was impossible for me now because with Christ, all things are possible! It is amazing how catching hold of that truth really changed my outlook on life. I knew that whatever God called me to do, I could do it because I wouldn't be doing it on my own.

So after much prayer, I took a leap of faith and quit my job. We wanted to build up our emergency fund first, so I gave a long advance notice, with my last day being February 18, 2011. It was just a random date that I picked. About a week after my last day of work, I found out I was pregnant with our third child. Most people thought we planned it that way. God did, we didn't!

It was a major adjustment going from being a working mom to a stay-at-home mom. My sons were two and one, and I was pregnant. I always enjoyed the beautiful baby that came after being pregnant, but I never enjoyed being pregnant. Being tired beyond tired and having to keep up with two energetic little boys was not easy. I felt like I dropped off the face of the earth because I hardly saw or talked to anyone anymore. I hungered for adult fellowship and to be able to share the love of God with others. But God was with me in the desert, and I used that time to get into the Word and learn more and more. The Word was just coming alive to me. But I constantly wondered what door God was going to open to get me started in my ministry. I couldn't see it yet, but I believed it would happen.

After almost two years of growing and learning, I felt God prompting me to write and share with others what I had learned. I felt very passionate about sharing the goodness of God and other truths because so many people seemed to have a wrong view of God. He directed me to contact the *Bargain Hunter* to see if I could write a column for them. It is a free advertising newspaper that is delivered to everyone in our county and some in surrounding counties. I didn't act immediately. I wanted to make sure it was truly from God and not just a personal desire. I knew that on my own I couldn't do it, and to be honest, it intimidated me to think about it.

But the desire lingered, so I called and left a message for the president of the paper, telling him my idea. That was a Friday. By Tuesday, I still hadn't heard anything. To be quite honest, I was a little relieved. But God told me to stick with it, so I decided to write an article and e-mail it to him. I did that on Tuesday afternoon, and he immediately wrote back, apologizing for not getting back to me sooner. He forwarded my article to the managing editor, who said she would get back to me. Then the waiting began. I had a mixture of emotions—excitement, fear, nervousness—yet within all those emotions was a deeper feeling of peace and rest. I know that may sound contradictory, but I don't know how to explain it any other way. When anxiety would start to flood my soul, I had to remind myself that God was in control of this one and I was just going to turn it over to Him and not worry about it.

A few days later, on Friday, she wrote back to me and said they decided to add me on as a writer. I still remember reading that in shock. *I'm going to be writing an article for a newspaper? Wow, this is way over my head. God, this is all You. You need to write through me. Without You leading and directing me, I am going to fall flat on my face!*

It has been a great experience for me. It is a passion of mine, and God has been so faithful. It has been about me allowing Him to work through me, trusting Him to give me the things to say and the way to say it. I pray in the Spirit a lot because I know I need the knowledge and revelation that only the Holy Spirit can give to me.

If you are reading this, let it serve as an encouragement to you. If God has called you to do something, don't let your own inadequacies stop you from doing what He has called you to. If He has called you, He will come through if you will allow Him to. I am living proof of that.

I hope you enjoy my articles and that they will reveal the goodness of God, His wonderful love for you, and the incredible sacrifice Jesus has made for us all. I have added some personal thoughts and feedback from readers at the end of the articles so you can see deeper into my heart and how the articles are touching others as well. God bless you. Enjoy!

Identity Crisis

Find Your Identity in Jesus Alone

Have you ever had an identity crisis? I have. Several times actually. Mine were subtle, I think most are, and I believe the vast majority of people, even Christians, battle with an identity crisis all the time.

What am I talking about? I am talking about deriving your self-worth from anything other than God. It's forming your opinion about yourself based on what you have achieved or what others think about you rather than what God thinks about you.

I used to get my self-worth from sports. From a very young age until my early twenties, sports played a major role in my life. I am not knocking sports; I think they are great, and I hope my boys end up being involved in them. But I let sports become who I was and what I was known for. I was the athlete. I wasn't the prettiest, smartest, most liked, or funniest, but I could play about any sport that had a ball involved and be decent at it. That was who I was and how I got attention.

If I had a bad game, I got very down on myself and beat myself up over every mistake. If I had a good game, I felt good about myself and welcomed the praise of people to build me up. My opinion of myself was up and down, depending on how I performed and what I thought people thought of me.

After my sports career was over, I entered the work force. Since I couldn't earn my identity from sports anymore, I then threw my weight into trying to achieve through my job. I was only there a few months when I earned the responsibility of handling a national account. I was proud of that. I put my whole heart into it and worked as hard as I could to see what else I could achieve. (On a side note, I think we should work as hard as we can; the Bible says we are to work unto the Lord.) I just wanted to keep climbing up that corporate ladder to make a name for myself. My self-worth was based on what I was achieving. How many of us fall into that trap?

After ten years of doing the same job (which was very humbling), I felt a call from God to be a stay-at-home mom. I obeyed the call. I didn't know how big of an adjustment that would be. It was a huge blow to my performance-based ego. Although I hadn't gotten the big promotion I had always dreamed of at my job, I did still derive my self-worth based on how well I did my job and always had something to work for.

Now I was left to change diapers, clean up messes, fight boys for naps, and just be a mom and housewife. I say *just* because that is how I felt, but there isn't a more important job than that! I can honestly say there is little to no recognition in it at all, and that was hard for me. I almost went into a depression at first. My thinking was, *Okay, God, what about me? What can I try to achieve now? What do I have to hope for? What goals can I aim for? I'm just stuck here at home.*

Although it has been and is still a struggle at times for me because it is exhausting work (I have all ornery boys, ages four, three, and one), I am so thankful that God called me to this and that I obeyed. I know I am exactly where God wants me to be right now. I have more time to read and study my Bible than ever before. I get the privilege of raising my three sons and telling them about a Jesus who loves them so much and wants good things for them. A word God has given me a few times is, "I never said it would be easy, but it will be worth it." And I believe that with all my heart.

I can see now how I got my worth from all the wrong places, and after almost two years of being at home, I am content with my role. I don't have to achieve or perform to feel good about myself anymore. The only place I look to get my identity is in Christ! And the only thing that truly brings peace is resting in the love of God, knowing that my Father loves me no matter what and I do not need to achieve for Him. Thank You, Lord!

I was overwhelmed by the positive feedback that I received after my first article came out in print. This is an edited version of what I had e-mailed to the president of the paper. It was very near to my heart because I know of some women who work so hard to excel in their career because it gives them a sense of importance. But we need to rely on Jesus to make us feel important.

Many people were shocked and caught off guard to see an article written by me in the paper since I had not told very many about this new opportunity. The response was very positive, and I believe a core group of readers was established through this article.

My Journey with God—Part 1

One of my favorite types of books to read is an autobiography. It helps me see into a person's life from their point of view, through their thoughts, feelings, and words. I get a true sense of who they are. I want you to get a true sense of who I am, and that is why I am going to share about myself. I shared a little bit in my last article, but there is much more to it than that. The following is about my journey with God. I hope it will help you to see more into my life and my relationship with God.

When I was young, around five or six, my dear grandma Lucy led my brother, cousin, and me to pray a prayer to get saved. I know she meant well, and I don't remember much about it, but I think the emphasis was staying out of hell, like it was our "get-out-of-hell free pass." I don't know if I really meant it in my heart, so I don't know if I truly became born again at that point or not.

Anyway, throughout my childhood, I had a little head knowledge of God, but not much heart knowledge. I saw Him as someone way out in the heavens somewhere, instead of someone personal who lived in my heart. I didn't know Him as the loving Heavenly Father that He really is.

At the age of seventeen, my senior year in high school, tragedy struck my family. My brother Matt was killed in a car accident. He was only twenty.

As you can imagine, his death brought complete devastation to my family. It left me as the only child now. I felt like I was living in a nightmare that I couldn't wake up from. Why did this have to happen to my brother, to my family? How would I ever recover from this? How would our family recover from this? Why did God allow this to happen? My dad was so badly hurt and broken through it all that he would never be the same.

Many people shared their opinions in hopes of comforting us, which at the time it did somewhat, but left me with the wrong view of God. "God needed another angel" or "God must have a purpose for doing this," and on and on it went. I accepted those things but got the wrong impression that everything that happens is God's will; He randomly does or allows bad things to happen to us, and you just never know about Him.

Matt's death was a wake-up call for me. I did end up committing my life to Christ and making Him my Lord after it, but not so much out of knowing His love and grace but rather out of fear. I knew my brother was saved, and I wanted to make sure I was too. I didn't want to go to hell and I wanted the hope of seeing my brother again someday.

Anyone else get saved that way? Out of fear of God's wrath instead of the abundance of God's love? Sad to say, I think it happens often.

I served God but also lived with a lot of guilt, fear, and confusion. Guilt because I had come to the conclusion that my brother died as a sacrifice for me and a few others for us to receive Christ. Fear because I thought if I "messed up," God might take someone else from me or do something bad to me to teach me a lesson. Confusion because if God is a good God, why does He have all these bad things happen?

To be continued.

There are many people who remember Matt's accident, either just by hearing of it or because they knew him or our family per-

sonally. I think hearing me put into words what I was dealing with touched many people. I received an even bigger response than the first article. I think there is something about sharing your deepest thoughts and feelings that draw people in. I put my article on Facebook, and many commented on how much they enjoyed and appreciated it.

One lady commented on my article on the Bargain Hunter's website that she couldn't wait to read part two because she had just lost her stepson in a car accident the day before, and she wanted to hear how I dealt with it. That touched me deeply. I realized at that point that God had given me this platform to reach many lives and proclaim His goodness to multitudes. It was a very humbling, sobering, yet exciting opportunity that I was eager to be able to follow with His leading.

My Journey with God—Part 2

I thought I had to do good to please God. I tried to do all the right things so that God wouldn't have reason to keep allowing bad things to happen to me. I was trying to earn His favor and approval. But bad things kept happening. *What is going on, Lord?* I thought. *The Bible says that You love me, but You really don't seem to like me very well!* Instead of feeling closer to God through hard times, He seemed more distant, and I didn't want to pray or fellowship with Him. But I knew I needed to keep that relationship with God because there was always that fear of falling away and going to hell, and that was the main reason I did so.

Then I started hearing and learning about the real God. The God who loves us unconditionally, not based on our performance. The God who would never cause or "allow" a tragedy or sickness to come upon us to teach us a lesson. The God who wants nothing but good things for us. The God who wants us well, not sick.

This seed of truth was first planted in me when my dad was dying of cancer. I don't know what would have happened if I thought God was the one who made my dad suffer so incredibly for six months. I probably would have kept serving Him like before, but my view of Him would have become more and more tainted. To see something like that happen to a loved one and then to hear people say that God was behind it, well, no wonder more people aren't Christians! Why would they want to serve a God like that?

I missed my dad terribly after his death, but I can't explain to you the peace in knowing that God wasn't the one who inflicted him with this awful disease or "allowed" it for some redemptive purpose. It came from our enemy, the devil, as did my brother's death. John 10:10 states, "The thief does not come except to steal, and to kill, and to destroy. I have come that they may have life, and that they may have it more abundantly." It came straight from the mouth of Jesus, and Jesus was the express image of God (Hebrews 1:3). Satan is out to steal, kill, and destroy, not God. God wants us to have an abundant life here on this earth, not just in eternity. God is for us and wants *only* good things for us. Isn't that a comfort? It sure is to me.

I now serve God out of love, not guilt or obligation. Joy, not fear. I am in awe of Him, and I hunger to fellowship with Him and to learn more and more about Him. The more I read my Bible now, the more it makes sense! I see how much He loves me and how much Christ really purchased for us on the cross!

The Bible says in John 8:32, "And you shall know the truth, and the truth will make you free." This is so true; the truth has set me free! Free from religious bondage and free to know how good of a God we truly serve! Free to know that things do happen out of the will of God and He isn't behind all the mayhem and suffering in the world.

I feel like such a different person since I have learned these things. There is much more I have learned as well, and I hope you will follow me in the future as I share some of these important truths.

I was rather disappointed after this article came out because there was much less response to this one than there was the first part, and I thought this article had the good stuff in it! I wanted people to see that God is good and bad things are not from Him.

I started to see that I would have a battle ahead of me because religion has blinded many people to the truth about God, and I was determined, with God and the Holy Spirit leading me, to get the word out about how truly good our God is.

A Conversation between God and Jesus

God: My Son, look at them. They need redemption; they need a Savior. There needs to be a sacrifice to take away their sins completely, not just cover them as the animal sacrifices do. It has to be the blood of a perfect man, not born with a sinful nature, to redeem mankind from what was lost in the garden.

Jesus, I wish there was another way, but there is not. Would You be that sacrifice? The word *sacrifice* doesn't give justice to what You will have to endure. You, being fully God, will become fully human as well. You, who created the universe and everything in it, will have to humble Yourself and become a servant to the people You have created. Some will love You, but many will despise You. The ones who will love You are those who know they are sinners and are hungry for a Savior. That was the purpose of the law, to show them they can never be good enough and they need a Savior. The law was to point them to You (Galatians 3:19, 24; Hebrews 10:1).

The ones that won't receive You and will despise You do so because of their own self-righteousness. They take pride in their flesh. They like having a set of rules to follow. They think they can earn their righteousness from their works. But no flesh will be justified in my sight by the deeds of the law (Romans 3:20).

You will be physically persecuted like no other persecution that ever has or will take place. You will not only be beaten worse than any other person, You will also be given the punishment for all the sins and iniquities of the entire world in Your physical body while carrying their sicknesses and infirmities as well (Isaiah 52:14; 53:3–4; Matthew 8:17). The chastisement for their peace will be upon You, and by Your stripes they will be healed (1 Peter 2:24, Isaiah 53:5). You will take their sinful nature on Your body and in return will give them Your righteousness (2 Corinthians 5:21). You will pay the price once and for all for *all* their past, present, and future sins (Hebrews 10:10, 12).

And at that point when You are hurting the most, all will forsake You, including myself (Mark 15:34). I will remove my spirit from You so You suffer the full effects of sin—separation from me. But that is only temporary, and soon You will be joined with Me at My right hand, and everything will be subject to You. (1 Peter 3:22, Hebrews 10:12).

You will be their ransom, and all that will be required on their part is to receive You by faith as their Lord (Ephesians 2:8–9). It is My will for all of them to receive You, but sadly that won't happen (1 Timothy 2:4, Matthew 7:13–14).

They will now be under My grace, no longer under the law (Romans 5:13). I will never be angry with them. I will never rebuke them. I will always have mercy on them. My kindness shall not depart from them, and My covenant of peace will never be removed (Isaiah 54:8– 10).

If they receive You, they will find favor and righteousness in My sight because of what *You* did, not because of what they do. That, my Son, is grace. It cannot be earned. It is My free gift to all who will believe.

Jesus, will You do it? Will You suffer and take the place for these people I love so much?

Jesus: I will do anything for them because I love them as much as You do. I come to do Your will, O God (Hebrews 10:9). Yes, Father, I will be their Savior.

This article took me a long time to write. I stressed over it because I wanted to tell the story of redemption in my own words and say it correctly. (I have learned more and more as I went along to rest in Jesus and not stress). I was excited to get to briefly introduce our freedom from the law and our new covenant of grace because of Jesus. I used a lot of scriptures because I wanted people to know this isn't just my opinion; it is truth revealed to us and for us in God's Word.

A woman named Shirley called and told me how much this article touched her and that she wanted her children to read it. She also reaffirmed that God had called me to write, and I was ever so thankful for her taking the time to call me and encourage me.

Perfect Love Makes Trusting Easy

My youngest son, Braxton, is about a year and a half and has been climbing up the stairs before he could walk. My husband taught him a few months ago how to go down the stairs, and now he is an old pro at it. But often, if I am there with him and I start to go down, he wants me to carry him. He stands there with his little arms outstretched and grunts. Since I am usually already down a few steps, I will reach out my arms to him and say, "Come." Then, that trusting little guy, with no hesitation, will simply fall forward into my arms. Practically every time he does so, I say to him, "Boy, you sure do trust your mommy." And every time I say that, I hear the spirit of God say to me, "I wish my children all trusted me like that." Wow. Powerful words, God.

So what is missing here? How is Braxton able to trust me so easily, without fear or reservation, yet it is hard for us to trust God? The answer: Braxton knows how much I love him. Simple as that. Why can't we trust God? The answer: we don't know how much He loves us.

In 1 John 4:18, it says, "There is no fear in love; but perfect love casts out fear, because fear involves torment. But he who fears has not been made perfect in love." To Braxton, my love is perfect. He knows how much I love him and I would never do anything to hurt him, so he can fully trust me with no fear. Now what if this little guy started doubting my love? He would think about what would happen if I didn't catch him and all the pain it could cause him to fall down the flight of steps. Not knowing my love for him could keep him from trusting me. He might decide to just crawl down the steps himself.

That would be a slap in the face to me! I would be heartbroken to think that my son didn't trust me. "Doesn't he know how much I love him? I would never do anything to hurt him, and I would put my own life at risk to make sure he wouldn't fall!" Bingo. Now we know how God feels! He loves us infinitely more than we are ever able to love anyone. Jesus didn't just risk His life because He loved us, but He actually *gave* His life for us all. When we can grasp how good Jesus is, how much He loves us, and what He did for us at the cross, worry and fear will go out the window and will be replaced with gratitude, trust, and confidence.

Now please don't feel condemned. There is no condemnation in Christ. We all need to get a better grasp of God's love.

I encourage you to get in the Word daily and read about the love God has for us. His word is His love letter to us. I also encourage you to pray daily for revelation of this love like Paul prayed in Ephesians 3:17–19: "That Christ may dwell in your hearts through faith; that you, being rooted and grounded in love, may be able to comprehend with all the saints what is the width and length and depth and height—to know the love of Christ which passes knowledge; that you may be filled with all the fullness of God."

I love that my son can trust me with his life; it is a beautiful reminder to me that if he can trust me that much, then I can trust my loving Heavenly Father because He loves me more than I could ever imagine.

God truly spoke to me every time that little guy would fall off the steps into my arms, yet I didn't know how to expand on it to bring out the depth of God's love. It didn't come to me all at once; so far each article, except the first one, has taken me hours to write. I realize how important praying in the Spirit is; I need the Holy Spirit's wisdom to be able to get the revelation of what to write.

A reader named Molly wrote, "This is an awesome article, Amber! Your words are so true, and I deeply needed to hear them."

Knowing Is Half the Battle

Allow me to share a scenario and see if it sounds familiar: People get born again. They are excited about Jesus. They feel and act changed and are on a spiritual high. But soon the newness and excitement wear off, and they think and feel like they did before they were saved. They ask themselves, "Does God love me? Was I really changed?" They wonder because they don't feel it anymore. They become defeated and dejected, thinking maybe they haven't really changed after all, and question their own salvation.

Have you ever seen this happen? I have, many times. And I have been there many times. Maybe you are in that situation now. Maybe you have given up because it just seems too hard to be a Christ follower. Please don't give up! The problem is a knowledge problem, or lack thereof. Finding out what actual transformation takes place on the inside of us when we are born again is the first step to living the abundant life Christ died for us to have.

Here is a verse you've probably heard many times: "Therefore, if anyone is in Christ, he is a new creation; old things have passed away; behold, all things have become new" (2 Corinthians 5:17). Our spirit is what this verse is referring to, not our body, mind, emotions, or feelings. That's what "born again" means: old things in our spirit pass away and all things in our spirit have become new. Our spirit has become a brand-new creation. Let me explain further.

Just like the Trinity is a three-part being in one (Father, Son, and Holy Spirit), we are as well. We are composed of body, soul, and spirit (See 1 Thessalonians 5:23.).

Our body is the physical part of us, the part we can see. Our soul is our mind and emotions, what we think and feel. Our spirit is our innermost being, the life-giving part of us, a part we can't see or feel. All of us had corrupted spirits because we were born with a sin nature. But because of Jesus, our wonderful Jesus, He took our old spirit that was corrupted by sin and in return gave us His spirit, His perfect, completely righteous spirit. I'll confirm this with a few scriptures.

> By this we know that we abide in Him, and He in us, because *He has given us His Spirit.* (1 John 4:13, italics mine)

> And because you are sons, *God has sent forth the Spirit of His Son into your hearts*, crying out, "Abba, Father!" (Galatians 4:6, italics mine)

> "For He made Him who knew no sin to be sin for us, that we might become the righteousness of God in Him." (2 Corinthians 5:21)

We are now the righteousness of God because of the sacrifice of Jesus on the cross. He literally traded places with us. He not only took our sin nature but in return gave us His righteous nature through His Spirit.

> Love has been perfected among us in this: that we may have boldness in the day of judgment; *because as He is, so are we in this world.*" (1 John 4:17, italics mine)

Do you choke on reading the last part of that verse? "I'm not like Jesus!" you exclaim. Well, maybe not in your body or soul, but in your spirit, you are! In our spirits, we are identical to Christ because He has taken our old spirit and given us His perfect spirit. Praise Jesus!

You may have never heard these things before. I know it is deep, but I encourage you to read it over a few times. Look up the scriptures for yourself and ask the Holy Spirit to reveal these truths to you. I want you to understand this because in my next article, I will explain the significance of it all and how to apply what we have learned so we can live a victorious and fulfilled Christian life.

One guy named Brad wrote, "Awesome job, Amber. I enjoy reading your articles."

A woman named Karen commented, "Can't wait. More exciting articles. Thanks, Amber!"

That was encouraging because I know the things I am writing are deep. I can start to see that some people are hungry to learn more and hear the deep things while others are not as hungry to dig into a deeper relationship with God.

Out with the Old and In with the New

In my last article, I talked about how when we are born again our old spirit is gone and has been recreated with the spirit of Jesus. So what is the significance of this, and how do we apply it to our Christian lives? The first point I want to make is that we need to now see ourselves as this new creation.

Ephesians 4:22–24 states, "That you put off, concerning your former conduct, the old man which grows corrupt according to the deceitful lusts, and be renewed in the spirit of your mind, and that you put on the new man which was created according to God, in true righteousness and holiness."

How do you put off the old man and put on the new man? Answer: in your mind. We need to put off (stop thinking about), the old corrupt person we used to be, and put on (start thinking about), the new person we are now in our spirit, created in true righteousness and holiness.

Most people have it the other way around. They think, "Okay, I am a Christian now, so I need to stop doing this and stop doing that. I need to put off those old actions." They try to control their actions and change their outside, but this won't last. True, lasting change has to start on the inside through knowing our new identity in Christ.

Proverbs 23:7 says, "For as he thinks in his heart, so is he." If you still see yourself as that dirty old sinner, you are still going to act like that dirty old sinner. But if you start seeing yourself as God sees you in your spirit because of Christ, you will start to act like the righteous person you are in your spirit. Right believing produces right actions.

You are not going to act differently from how you think about yourself.

Instead of thinking of yourself as just an old sinner saved by grace, say, "I was an old sinner, but praise God, not anymore. Now I am saved by grace because of Jesus! I am righteous because of Jesus!" Being sin-conscious makes us self-focused while being righteousness-conscious makes us Jesus-focused. We definitely want to be Jesus focused! (See Isaiah 26:3.)

I encourage you to practice this. See yourself as a completely new creation, completely forgiven. See yourself as the righteousness of God in Christ Jesus. Not righteous because of your works, but righteous because Jesus died to make you righteous. Your works can never make you righteous; it is all because of Jesus.

If you have trouble with this, I want to ask you to picture something with me. If you have watched *The Passion of the Christ* or the recent Bible miniseries, you have seen the brutal beatings that Jesus had to incur (and I believe it was much worse that what they were able to depict). Think of that now. Think of Jesus being beaten and whipped, with a crown of thorns placed on His brow. Picture Him barely able to walk, needing help to carry that heavy cross up the hill. Then see them pounding the nails through His hands and feet, and lifting the cross up with Him on it. Envision yourself up there, face-to-face with Jesus, looking into His eyes that are filled with nothing but love for you and me. Then hear Him whisper to you, "I took your sin, so you could become righteous with our Father through Me (2 Corinthians 5:21). I did it for you. It's already paid for. Please receive My grace."

I hope that helped you to see it a little better. When we don't think of ourselves this way, we are basically saying that the sacrifice of Jesus wasn't enough to make us righteous. My friends, His sacrifice was everything!

I am very passionate about this. This simple truth of knowing who I am in the spirit has been life-changing for me. I have more to share, so this will be continued.

I got very little feedback on this article, so it was a little disappointing because I think it is something that people need to hear and understand. Too many people have a wrong opinion of who they are because they don't know what Jesus has truly done for them.

Father, may Your Son be glorified in every article I write. May I point others to His amazing sacrifice for us all.

Learning to Walk in the Spirit by Faith

In my last two articles, we have learned what happens to our spirit when we are born again and that we should see ourselves as God sees us in the spirit. Now I want to show how to learn to walk in that spirit, rather than living by how we feel.

First, we need to know what is in our spirit. Remember, your spirit is the part of you that you can't feel. Since we can't feel or see our spirit, how do we know what is in it? Through the Word of God. The Word is our spiritual mirror. Just like we don't know what we look like unless we look in a mirror, we don't know what our spirit looks like until we look in the Bible to tell us. The more we get into and meditate on the Word, the more revelation we get of who we are in the spirit, and it becomes more real to us.

Secondly, we need to renew our mind to these truths. Romans 12:2 states "And do not be conformed to this world, but be transformed by the renewing of your mind, that you may prove what is that good and acceptable and perfect will of God."

How do we become transformed? By the renewing of our mind. What are we to renew our minds to? The Word of God. The Word of God can literally transform you without you even realizing it when you constantly meditate on the promises of God rather than have your mind on the things of the world.

I can tell you, very rarely are you going to feel the way the Word talks about you. This is where faith comes in. It takes faith to believe in what you can't see or feel about yourself. Second Corinthians 5:7 says, "For we walk by faith, not by sight." This isn't just talking about physical sight but anything we can perceive with our five senses. It could say, "For we walk by faith, not by how we feel." *You won't feel the incredible qualities that are in your spirit; you need to accept it by faith, the same way you do your salvation.*

I can say from personal experience that these truths work. I wouldn't be writing this if I didn't know that they did. But I don't do this perfectly and doubt I ever will. To the degree that I renew my mind and meditate on the word of God is the degree that I will walk in victory. It isn't just a once-a-day thing, but it needs to be a constant way of life. This is so vitally important.

"You're a stay-at-home mom," you might say. "You have more time to do that. I have a job that I need to focus on." Even at work, you can find time to worry, can't you? I worked before I was a stay-at-home mom, and yes, I know this is true. Replace those thoughts with the promises of God. Do you ever think of the big game you watched last night or the one you can't wait to watch when you get home? That mind can be used to meditate on the Word. It is a choice. You can't prevent a thought from coming in, but you can decide whether you will give it priority to occupy your mind or not.

I've talked a lot about getting into the Word, and in many future articles, I will share what some of these incredible promises and truths about us from the Bible actually are. It is exciting to me, and I hope it will be to you too!

Renewing our mind to these truths is so important. It isn't something that just happens; we need to constantly make it a priority. It can be hard living in this world and having the world pull us in all different directions, but we need to make renewing our mind to the truths of God's Word a focal point.

Karen wrote, "Again you give me so much to think about!"

Keep Your Eyes on the Prize

My oldest son, AJ, is four, and my middle son, Grady, is three. To say they have a lot of energy is, well, an understatement. I had a brilliant idea the other day of a way they could burn off some of that built-up energy and exercise their competitive natures. Why not race across our yard? My suggestion fell on ready ears. The race entailed running to the playset, touching it, and coming back to the swing I was sitting on.

Now let me explain my boys. Both are tall for their age, but they are built so differently. AJ is long and lean like his daddy while Grady is more stout. (That word makes me think of my dad because he used to say it about me). AJ is a natural runner with his long smooth strides, but Grady has to put more effort into it (he must get that from me also). Not that he is slow, AJ is just fast.

I decided to give Grady a head start to make it more fair. "On your mark, get set, go!" I shouted. AJ immediately took off while Grady was slow to get going. I think by the time Grady started running, AJ had already passed him. It was no contest. AJ won by a landslide.

So the next time, I gave Grady a very generous lead to start. But this time, he was so focused on AJ, who was behind him, that he lost sight of the target ahead of him. He kept turning around and looking for AJ, and once A.J. caught up to him, Grady tried to push him so he couldn't pass him, all the while failing to run in a straight line, making the distance to the goal a little longer. AJ won again.

Before the next race, I motioned Grady over to have a talk with him. "Listen, buddy," I said. "You can win. Don't think about AJ. You just run straight to the playset and come straight back. Just do that and don't worry about AJ, okay?"

I gave an even bigger head start to Grady this time. *He's going to finally beat AJ*, I thought to myself. They took off as I yelled go, but Grady seemed to forget all about our little pep talk. Once again, his focus was on AJ, *once again turning around, zigzagging from side to side, not focused on the prize but rather distracted by the obstacle that stood in his way of victory.* Once again he lost and was disappointed.

Oh how I wanted him to finally win one. I kept thinking how he could have won if he would have just kept his eyes on the goal instead of on the distractions around him. But did I really expect my three-year-old to understand this concept that we as adults struggle with? We are constantly bombarded with situations, circumstances, and people vying for our attention. It is so easy to focus on those things instead of the One who gives us the power to achieve our victory. Will we keep our eyes and mind on the prize (Jesus) or allow those distractions to keep us from living the abundant life that God has called us to?

I believe God is like I was, that loving parent, cheering us on, wanting us to win every race or battle that we come up against. I picture Him saying, "I want you to win. I know the plan of how to. Lay aside every weight, every sin, and every distraction that competes for your attention. Keep your eyes focused on My Son. Then you will win!" (Hebrews 12:1–2, my paraphrase).

What race or battle are you in today? Know that God is on your side, and the key to victory is staying focused on Jesus!

I remember sitting on that swing, watching those two precious little boys racing. The Holy Spirit started prompting me to write an article on it. Okay, God, I can write the part that I see of them racing. It is up to you to reveal to me the ending. And He did! God is definitely our biggest fan and is always cheering us on, wanting the best for us in every situation.

What Does the Fruit of the Spirit Really Mean?

I remember a time I was talking to a friend of mine. I know I was struggling with having patience. What I was impatient about, I don't remember. My part of the conversation isn't clear, but I distinctly remember his words. He told me, "Remember, the fruit of the spirit is patience."

"Yeah, I know," I replied. But looking back, I really had no idea what that meant. I knew I should have it, so I tried in my flesh to be patient, but that didn't work. What I didn't know was that I already had it in my spirit!

Galatians 5:22 reads, "But the fruit of the Spirit is love, joy, peace, long-suffering (patience), kindness, goodness, faithfulness, gentleness, self-control. Against such there is no law."

All those amazing qualities, qualities that we usually beg and plead with God to give us, are already in our born again spirit! He has already given it to us through Jesus. Isn't that incredible?

Okay, so you're probably thinking I have gone crazy. If I had patience already inside of me, wouldn't I feel it? *No, because it is in my spirit, and that is the part of us we can't feel, but we accept it by faith because the Word of God says so.* The more we meditate on all the fruits of the spirit and the fact that we already have them, the more they will become real to us and we will see them manifest outwardly in our lives as visible fruit.

I can tell you, I am not naturally a patient person. I am not the laid-back, calm, anything-goes type of person. But

I know now that I have a new nature, and I need to focus on who I am in my new, born-again spirit. I have to remind myself that I am a new creation; that old person is gone, and in my spirit, I have all the patience I will ever need.

Let me tell you, most days it takes a load of patience to handle my three ornery, rambunctious boys! I don't do this perfectly, so please don't think that I think I do. I have a *long* way to go. There are days when I am not focusing on the Word and who I am in the spirit that I think to myself, "I just can't handle this! I need help!" In those times, I am relying on my flesh, my own strength, instead of drawing from the *abundance* of what is in my spirit. But when I renew my mind to who I am in Christ and all that is in me in my spirit, I can draw from the well of patience inside of me when a situation arises that requires it. I don't always feel like doing this, that's for sure. My flesh, the carnal part of me, usually wants to lose it. ("The flesh lusts against the spirit and the spirit against the flesh," [Galatians 5:17]). I give in to my feelings more often than I would like. But when I am in tune to my spirit and know that I don't have to go by how I feel, I say to myself, "I have patience in my spirit. I am not trying to get it. It is already inside of me because Jesus died to give it to me. I choose to walk in patience. I can do all things through Christ who gives me strength," and bingo, I am walking in the spirit rather than the flesh, not giving into my feelings.

This is a simple truth, but it isn't going to come instantly or easily. It takes effort, but the effort isn't doing it in and of ourselves but relying on God, meditating on His word, and drawing from what we already have in our spirit. You will mess up, but don't get condemned when you do. God isn't condemning you. He loves you and is your biggest fan. You can do all things through Christ who gives you strength!

One lady in church told me how she read this article over many times. She said it caused her to realize that she already had all those things inside of her, and she wasn't trying to get God to give them to her.

Praise God that some are getting this! May others understand it as well. This is a topic that you don't really hear people talk about, but I think it is an essential foundation to our identity in Christ.

Don't Limit What God Is Able to Do through You

Let me ask you a question: do you think you can limit God? I can just hear "no" resonating as people read this. No, of course you can't limit God. He is all-powerful, nothing can limit God.

Well, I hate to burst your bubble, but that is not true. God is all-powerful in that there is no one more powerful than Him, but did you know that we can limit God? Before you get mad and dismiss this article, stick with me, and I will explain.

Psalms 78:41 clearly states, "Yes, again and again they tempted God, and limited the Holy One of Israel." Right there, it is saying that the people of Israel limited God. How did they limit God? By their small thinking. The next few verses after that mention how they forgot His power and all the miraculous things He did to bring them out of Egypt. *They limited what He could do through them because of their unbelief.*

We limit God as well. God wants to move through us more than we know. But we have to let Him. God has great plans for all of us, not just a select few here and there.

One of my favorite verses is Ephesians 3:20, "Now to Him who is able to do exceedingly abundantly above all that we ask or think, *according to* the power that works in us" (italics mine). I italicized that to emphasize how God is able to do these marvelous things. Most people quote the first part of the verse and leave out the last half. I think they do so because it puts it all back on God. "Oh yes, God can do whatever He wants, whenever He wants," they say, and it takes us out of the picture. It makes God out to be this mysterious being that you just don't know about; maybe you will be the chosen one that He wants to do amazing things for. But God wants amazing things for *all* of us!

The way God is able to do exceedingly abundantly beyond all we ask or think is through His power working in us. It is a joint effort between us and God. Isn't that amazing? It is His power, but we are the vessels that He chooses to work through. Our part is to believe and receive this incredible power by faith and allow God to work through us.

I meditate on this verse all the time. It reminds me of how much God is able to do through me because of His power living in me. It should remind you how much God is able to do through you as well.

It would be incredible if He could just do all that we ask or think. It would be awesome if He could do *above* all we ask or think. But, no, He wanted to make His point very clear—He is able to do *exceedingly abundantly above* all we ask or think through His power in us. "Don't limit God" resonates from this verse.

Have you ever gone there in your mind? Have you ever thought that our amazing, powerful, loving God has put His power in us and everything is possible? Did you know we have the same power on the inside of us that raised Jesus from the dead?

Paul prays an incredible prayer for the people of Ephesus. Part of that prayer is for them to know what incredible power they have as believers. Ephesians 1:19–20 says, "And what is the exceeding greatness of His power toward us who believe, according to the working of His mighty power which He worked in Christ when He raised Him from the dead and seated Him at His right hand in heavenly places."

I encourage you to write down Ephesians 1:19–20 and Ephesians 3:20. Meditate on those verses until the power that is inside of you as a born-again believer becomes real in your heart, not just in your head. When that happens, you will quit limiting God by your small thinking, and nothing will be impossible for you!

Jess wrote, "Great job, Amber. This is so relevant and something we don't think about very often."

A guy at church told me he enjoyed reading my articles and that they were very easy to read, just like I was talking to him. I took that as a major compliment and told him I am a pretty simple person and don't use big words, so I do write the way I talk.

Boy, I want people to think about this! What power we have been given through the blood of Jesus. If Christians caught hold of that, we could change the world!

God Chooses the Foolish Things of the World

"For you see your calling, brethren, that not many wise according to the flesh, not many mighty, not many noble, are called. But God has chosen the foolish things of the world to put to shame the wise, and God has chosen the weak things of the world to put to shame the things which are mighty; and the base things of the world and the things which are despised God has chosen…that no flesh should glory in His presence" (1 Corinthians 1:26–29).

I love those verses. The reason is because they qualify me to be used by God! I am not what people of the world would consider wise or mighty. I think I would be considered foolish according to them. The Bible is my guide, not what the latest newsperson, Hollywood star, or psychiatrist says. I know that I don't have any ability in and of myself that makes me able to do great things on my own.

God chooses people who are weak and in themselves know they are nothing, because those people are the ones that have to rely on God to bring whatever they are called to do to pass. Then who gets the glory? God.

Many people have a God-given talent—it may be intelligence, athletic ability, and so on. But most people with these natural abilities are not called to serve God in the area they are gifted in because they tend to rely on their own natural ability instead of relying on God. Then they get the glory instead of God.

I heard of a guy who had a great voice and used to sing in bars before he was saved. Then he got born again and was excited because he thought he could now sing for God. He quit singing in bars, but God didn't call him to sing for Him right away. This guy was confused. Years later, after he matured in his walk with the Lord and realized his dependence on God, God called Him to sing. He discovered he wasn't called earlier because he would have trusted in his own ability rather than relying on God to work through him.

Let me tell you, writing an article is beyond my natural ability. Some people are naturally gifted as writers; I am not. When God first put this in my heart to write a column, I struggled with the idea. "God, I am not a writer," I argued. "I am not able to do this." But God said, "You're right. You are not a writer on your own. But you aren't on your own. I'm not calling you to rely on yourself to do it. I am calling you to rely on me. If you rely on me, you can do it."

Then Ephesians 3:20 came to me, which says that "God is able to do exceedingly, abundantly beyond all we ask or think, according to the power that works in us." It made me realize that I don't want to limit what God can do through me. God is able to do much more through me than I can even imagine because it is His power living on the inside of me. I renew my mind to this verse often. When I start thinking I can't do this whole writing thing or anything else, I think of that verse and remind myself that I am not doing it on my own, and I need to depend entirely on God to work through me.

What has God called you to do that you think you don't qualify for? Be encouraged! You are a prime candidate to be used by God. If you rely on Him, and not your own natural ability, nothing that God has called you to do will be impossible for you! And the best part? God will get the glory!

WorkingAmerican wrote on the paper's website: "Love this article. Will be sharing."

The truth that I have relayed through this article is how I am able to do what I am doing. If I start looking at natural talent and ability, I disqualify myself. I can't do it on my own and have to rely on the Holy Spirit to do it through me. When I struggle to write, I just have to sit back and allow God to work through me because on my own, I can't do this.

What I Have Learned about Grieving

I am writing this on Friday, June 7. What is the significance of this date? It was seven years ago today that my dad passed away.

November 3 is also a significant date in our family because it is the anniversary of my brother's death. This year it will be eighteen years since the car accident that took his life.

I was reminiscing today on how much I have changed in handling these dates. I thought I would pass along what I have learned and perhaps it might help someone.

It used to be that when the date of my brother's death was approaching, I thought I had to start the grieving and mourning process all over again. In my eyes, in order to do my brother justice, I had to make myself miserable. I was reliving the nightmare over again. I would make myself think and hash over all the events that took place. How I got the call at my friend Travis', the ride to the hospital with my mom and dad when we didn't yet know the outcome, the doctor telling us in the little private room about his death, and then seeing him lying in the hospital bed lifeless. I would just meditate on all those things over and over again. I thought if I wasn't miserable, I wasn't properly paying tribute to my brother. And believe me, I was miserable. That sick feeling in the pit of my stomach returned, and the wounds that had started to slowly heal were ripped open again.

During my dad's sickness, I started learning more about how good God is and that He wants good things for us. My mind-set has changed so much since Matt's death. Before,

I had a sense of guilt if I wasn't always thinking of him. But now I know this guilt I was feeling wasn't from God. God doesn't want me to be miserable or to feel guilty if I don't think about my dad or brother twenty-four hours a day. When I am thinking about them, I can't be thinking about Him. God has taught me I can still love and miss my loved ones without it having to consume me or always occupying my thoughts. And there is no guilt in that! Does that mean I don't miss my dad or brother? Of course not!

Philippians 4:8 says, "Whatever things are true, whatever things are noble, whatever things are just, whatever things are pure, whatever things are lovely, whatever things are of good report, if there is any virtue and if there is anything praiseworthy—meditate on these things." This is an awesome verse. Notice that it doesn't say to meditate on all the bad things that have happened to you, which is what most people tend to do. I could easily fall into depression if I would focus on how many people I loved dearly are no longer with me; so many people who never got to meet my dear husband or precious children.

I believe a lot of people could get out of depression if they would just do what these verses say. We get depressed because we are thinking about all that is wrong instead of right.

God wants us to think about the positive, not the negative. Thinking negative will conjure up negative emotions. Thinking positive will bring positive emotions. Our emotions are tied to what we think about.

So now, instead of grieving and focusing on what I have lost, I try to focus on what has been gained. My dad and brother are reunited in heaven, getting to fellowship with each other and with our loving Heavenly Father, and I will get a chance to see them again some day. And for that I am so very thankful.

I still remember getting the inspiration for this article. I had a hard time sleeping one night, so I ended up on the couch in the living room. As I woke up, I remembered what day it was, and I recounted how much things had changed in my life in regard to those anniversary dates. It no longer had to be a day of mourning for me. I didn't have to make myself miserable. I could remember without having to get depressed. This was one article that didn't take me long to write.

This is the article I probably received the most feedback on. One of my friends sent me a text saying that her dad wanted her to relay a message that he always likes reading my articles, but he especially liked this one. I received a card in the mail from a lady in town that knew my dad well. She said this was a beautiful article, and it touched her. I think I got so much feedback because many people knew my Dad and brother and were encouraged to see how I was dealing with the tragedies in my life. Hopefully it gave them a better outlook on how to deal with theirs as well.

What Is the True Meaning of Grace?

There are many Bible words and terms that I think people use and throw around without actually knowing the true meaning of them. I believe the word *grace* is one of them. You hear it used all the time. "The grace of God," "saved by grace," and so on.

So what does God's grace really mean? My friend asked me that a few months ago. What would you say? I am by no means an expert on the subject, but I have learned a lot about it the past few years and will do my best to explain what I have learned.

Grace is the unearned, undeserved, unmerited favor of God. Did you get that?

Unearned, undeserved, unmerited favor of God. This means that no amount of good works or good deeds or right living makes us deserving of grace. We should never be under the assumption that we have earned or could earn the favor of God. We could never be good enough. Grace is given to us because of the work of Jesus, not because of us. We were not worthy of Him to take our place on the cross, but He took our place and bore our sins because He loves us.

He didn't just take our place to spare us punishment; He also took our place to give us favor with God. Does that sound too good to be true?

It is true. That is the love of our Savior.

We are no longer under the law but are now living in the age of grace (Romans 6:14). God is not judging us for our sins because He already judged Jesus for them on the cross. We don't have to earn the favor of God through our works;

we *have* the favor of God because of Jesus. Our part is to receive this grace by faith.

I remember a few years ago when a friend of mine was struggling in his spiritual walk. He was actually mad at God because he thought he was doing everything right and God hadn't done anything for him. I didn't know what to say to him. I didn't have a deep understanding of grace. He didn't understand grace either, because in essence he was saying, "Okay, God, I've done my part. I have worked hard and done things worthy of Your blessings. When are you going to come through for me and do Your part?"

He had a works mind-set. A lot of people do. I did! That is not grace. God doesn't do things for us because He owes us; He does things for us because He loves us. Grace can never be earned. If you try to earn it, you fall from grace. Romans 4:4 says, "Now to him who works, the wages are not counted as grace but as debt."

Grace might be hard to grasp because it is opposite of the world's system. The world's system says you have to work hard and earn everything and nothing is ever free.

In contrast, God's grace says you can't earn it—don't even try—just receive it freely by faith. There is that innate part of us that thinks this can't be possible. People don't treat us that way. That's right. People don't, but Jesus does. Jesus is love overflowing to people who don't deserve it.

I encourage you to meditate on the true meaning of grace, the unearned, undeserved, unmerited favor of God.

When I do this, which I try to quite often, it causes me to shake my head in awe and wonder and say with a heart overflowing with gratitude, "Thank You, thank You, thank You, Lord!"

I remember one older woman in town telling me that this was her favorite article. Another lady that I didn't know wrote me on Facebook, telling me how much she enjoyed it as well.

Understanding grace (which is the whole concept of the new covenant) has truly transformed my life. Instead of it being about what I have to do for God, it is all about what God has done for me through Jesus. Oh what a difference from what I used to believe! And it is not because I deserve it, which makes it so much more special. It is because I didn't *deserve it that causes love and thanksgiving to abound in my heart for my incredible Savior.*

People need to truly get a grasp on grace. I believe there is a grace revolution that is starting to take place in this world, and that is awesome news!

We Are in a Spiritual Battle, and the Battle Is in Your Mind

I'm going to be brutally honest here.

Last weekend, I did the exact thing I wrote about in a previous article *not* to do. For the sake of space, I will not go into all the details, but basically I was throwing a pity party for myself. My husband was gone on a work trip for the weekend, and I was left alone to take care of our boys. I was looking at what was wrong, instead of concentrating on all that was right.

At one point, my father-in-law called and told me that he and my mother-in-law were thinking of me and that they know it is hard on me when Mike is gone. I started crying, verbalizing to him the pity party I had been having in my mind. I am so thankful he spoke the truth to me. Basically he said, "I know it is hard. But don't let yourself go there. Don't go down that path and think about all the negative things and that no one cares. Don't give in to Satan. Start thinking about what is good and be thankful."

Do you think that is what my flesh wanted to hear? No. But is that what I needed to hear? Absolutely. After hearing his words, I knew I had a choice. I could either keep doing what I was doing, feeling sorry for myself and indulging my flesh, or I could choose a different path. I could choose to get my eyes off myself and think about Jesus and how much I am blessed.

I am happy to say that I chose the better road. I decided I was not going to let Satan win that battle. James 4:6 says,

"Therefore submit to God. Resist the devil, and he will flee from you."

I had not been resisting the devil. I was giving in to him and all the lies he was trying to feed me. When I started getting my mind off myself and onto Jesus and all that He not only did for me on the cross but also has given to me here on earth through His grace, my feelings and countenance changed. The tears were gone, and a smile appeared. I started seeing my sons as the blessings that they are.

I think God wants to use me to speak to someone right now who is battling depression. Just like I needed reminded that I had a choice in the matter, you need to know that as well. I want to speak the truth in love because it is only the truth that will set you free (John 8:32).

We are in a spiritual battle, and the battle is in your mind. Your thoughts are the key to your peace. The devil will plant thoughts in your head, but you don't have to let them stay there. He wants you to be depressed; he wants you to keep your mind on yourself and your problems and off of Jesus because he knows in Jesus you will find peace. Isaiah 26:3 says, "You will keep him in perfect peace, whose mind is stayed on You, because he trusts in You." The key to walking in peace is focusing on Jesus.

Meditate on what you know is true in your spirit from the Word rather than focusing on how you feel and your circumstances. Jesus came that you may have life and have it more abundantly (John 10:10). God wants you to have hope (Jeremiah 29:11). You have the spirit of the living God living inside of you, and in your spirit is peace and joy! (Galatians 5:22–23).

If you renew your mind to these things and know the fact that Jesus loves you more than you will ever know, your feelings will change. It may not be instantly, but it will happen if you keep your thoughts on Jesus. Don't let the enemy steal from you any longer. Spiritual-mindedness produces life and peace (Romans 8:6). It is a battle. Believe me, I know, but don't be condemned or discouraged. You are more than a conqueror (Romans 8:37) and can do *all things* through Christ who gives you strength!

Nathan wrote, "Thanks for the column…right on target!! Another good one…I enjoy reading them."

Our thoughts are so important. I think our moods fluctuate depending on what we think about. We need to train our minds to stay focused on Jesus and not on how we feel. Lord, help me in this area!

A Free Gift Is a Blessing to Be Received

The other day, I decided to load the boys in the van and venture across town to my friend Jill's garage sale. (This may sound like an adventure, but I live in Baltic, so it only took me a minute. Literally.) After looking around, I found a few small items I wanted to purchase. As I laid them on the table to pay, her neighbor and friend, Abby, was tending the money table. She noticed I was buying her stuff and remarked, "Oh, you can just have them."

Instantly, I said, "Oh no, I'll pay you for them."

"No, really, just take them," she replied.

"Well, let me give you something for it," I said, fumbling through my wallet.

And her reply was a classic, one that I think people should use much more often. "Don't steal my blessing from me!" she retorted with a smile.

"Okay, I receive your blessing," I said. "Thank you!"

That made an impression on me. Why is it so hard for us to receive things when people are trying to bless us? When she first said I could have the items, even though it only would have cost me a couple of dollars at the most, it was like these sirens went off in my head, blaring, "You don't deserve it! You can't just receive that from her without giving her anything in return. Give her something for it!"

Her reply put me in my place. She just wanted to be a blessing, and if I wouldn't have let her give me the items, I would have taken away the joy that she received from being a blessing. I think we do this all the time. Someone wants to be a blessing, and we struggle with just receiving what they want to give us. "Well, I have to do something for them now," we think, instead of just receiving with a grateful heart. I know I have been on the other end as well; when I want to do something nice for someone, either they won't receive it or later think they have to give me something back in some way.

I think we do this with God as well. God *wants* to bless us, with no strings attached, but we struggle with receiving because we think we are undeserving or need to earn it. But remember what grace is? The unearned, undeserved, unmerited favor of God. That is what God has given to us through Jesus, and it isn't because we did anything to deserve it.

Romans 5:15 states, "But the free gift is not like the offense. For if by the one man's offense many died [talking about Adam's sin in the garden], much more the grace of God and the gift by the grace of the one Man, Jesus Christ, abounded to many."

God's grace is abounding to us. Isn't that awesome? His unmerited favor is overflowing toward us, but just like I had to receive Abby's gift of the garage sale items, we also have to receive Jesus's gift of grace by faith. Romans 5:2 says, "Through whom also we have access by faith into the grace in which we stand, and rejoice in hope of the glory of God." Faith reaches out and takes through believing what Jesus has already provided by grace.

Although I could have paid for the garage sale items, Jesus's gift on the cross could never be repaid. Our job is to not try to repay Him but to say by faith something like this: "Thank you, Jesus, for your sacrifice. Thank you for your grace that has been poured out to all who believe in You as our Savior. There is nothing I have done to deserve Your unmerited favor, but I thank You that You are so loving that You give us what we don't deserve. Jesus, I want to receive all the blessings that You died on the cross to give me. Thank You, Lord!"

Why is it so easy to give to others but hard to receive from them? I still struggle with it, but I try to remind myself that I like to give to others so I need to be able to receive from others as well. It isn't because I deserve it, but rather it is just a gift that someone wants to use to bless me.

I had a lady come up to me and tell me that she enjoys my articles, and she especially liked this one. She said her family had been invited by someone to go to their place for vacation and to do it free of charge. She was struggling to accept because she didn't think she deserved it. After reading this article, she realized that she didn't deserve it, but someone wanted to bless her anyway, so they went on the trip and had a great time.

Thank You, Lord, for using me to touch Your children. I am deeply humbled. It is all about You!

God Is Not to Blame

In this article, I want to attempt to disprove a doctrine that is so prevalent today. One that I believe has turned many people away from God and has led to a wrong representation of what He is really like. It is something I think Satan has brought into the church in his subtle way to blind people to what God is really like. It is a doctrine that I used to believe and promote.

I thought God controlled everything and nothing could happen that wasn't His will. So every time something bad happened, I started reasoning in my mind why God would have allowed this. I would think about what I must have done wrong and what God was trying to teach me. Or I would find one little good thing that came out of it, and I would conclude that was the reason God had it happen.

Let me be the first to tell you: that is not true! God doesn't control everything. Things do happen out of the will of God, and if something bad happens, it isn't God who is behind it. God wants good things for us, not bad. Here is a simple yet profound truth I want you to remember: God equals good; Satan equals bad. If we would adhere to that logic, so many questions would be answered. The blame would be taken off God and placed where it really belongs.

Scripturally, it isn't hard to prove that things happen out of the will of God. Just look at Adam and Eve. Do you think God wanted them to sin in the garden? Absolutely not! He told them not to eat of the tree of the knowledge of good and evil. It was their choice because they were given a free will. Did they eat of that tree? Yes. So we can conclude just from that instance that things happen out of the will of God. But I will give you more examples.

Second Epistle of Peter 3:9 states, "The Lord is not slack concerning His promise, as some count slackness, but is long-suffering towards us, not willing that any should perish but that all should come to repentance." First Timothy 2:3–4 reads, "For this is good and acceptable in the sight of God our Savior, who desires all men to be saved and to come to the knowledge of the truth."

Both of those verses are saying that it is God's will for all people to be saved. God doesn't want anyone to go to hell. He has lovingly provided through His Son's sacrifice the opportunity for anyone to receive the gift of eternal life. But do all receive this? Sadly, no. So once again, we can conclude that things happen out of the will of God.

Deuteronomy 30:19 says, "I call heaven and earth as witnesses today against you, that I have set before you life and death, blessing and cursing; therefore choose life, that both you and your descendants may live." Here, God is giving a choice. He is even giving the answer, but it is still up to us to make decisions for ourselves. Our decisions can go against the will of God.

Examples of things happening out of the will of God are all throughout the Bible.

Will some reject this even though the Bible proves it? Yes. Will some get mad at me for sharing this? Yes. I have experienced both to large degrees, and I believe it is because traditions and doctrines of man have made the word of God of no effect. (Mark 7:13, my paraphrase)

Maybe you have been taught that God controls everything and have never heard anything different. I am asking you to keep an open mind to the Holy Spirit directing you to the truth about our good God.

To be continued.

※

This topic is very near to my heart. Before I learned the truths in this article and the next few following ones, I was completely blinded to what God is really like. I cannot tell you the freedom *in knowing that God is good and that the bad things that happen are not His will. I know this is a touchy subject, and I asked God to help me boldly share these truths because so few people know it but need to know it. I was happy that people seemed to receive this message.*

Andy wrote, "Well done, Amber!"

Bertie wrote, "You are fully correct, Amber! Great job explaining the will of God!"

Sean wrote, "Great words, Amber, and good examples on how God gives us freedom of choice. If free will didn't exist, then there would be no need for salvation and grace. I look forward to reading more."

Every Good and Perfect Gift Is from Above

It seems to me that many people seem to base the doctrine of God controlling everything on Job. Now I am by no means an expert on Job, so I don't want to get into it too much. But I can tell you that God isn't sitting at a desk in heaven while Satan approaches Him for His permission to wreak havoc on God's children, and God either says, "Okay, go ahead" or "No, not this time." I think many people have this view of God. Let me give you a verse that throws that whole logic out the window.

First of all, we have a covenant now with God through the blood of Jesus. Through this new covenant, God says in James 1:13, "Let no one say when he is tempted, 'I am tempted by God'; for God cannot be tempted by evil, nor does He himself tempt anyone."

Wow, did you get that? *God cannot be tempted by evil, nor does he himself tempt anyone.* Thinking that Satan has to come to God and get His permission to do evil is absolutely false. It cannot and does not happen. God *cannot* be tempted by evil, nor does He tempt anyone.

God even knew that people would be deceived into believing this wrong doctrine because He said a few verses later in verses 16–17: "Do not be deceived, my beloved brethren. Every good gift and every perfect gift is from above, and comes down from the Father of lights, with whom there is no variation or shadow of turning."

I am telling you, just like the Bible states, do not be deceived! God only gives good gifts. God doesn't cause or allow all these tragedies going on. God only gives good gifts!

A friend I went to high school with contacted me a few months ago about a situation she was in. One of her best friends had been shot and killed by her husband, and then he turned the gun on himself, all this happening in front of one of their daughters. Wow, what a complete act of evil. The reason she contacted me was because she knew I had been through some tough times and wondered if I had some scriptures that gave me comfort that I could share with her, which she could in turn share with the girls.

The first thing I shared with her was that this horrifying act was not from God; it was from Satan. God was grieving for those girls and never wanted to see them going through what they were. I felt such a strong desire to really share the truth because I knew people would be blaming God for this. And her exact words back to me were, "That's exactly what everyone keeps telling me; that God has a reason for allowing this to happen. And it has made me angry. I even found myself not praying because I felt so much hurt and anger. I know how I feel and can't even imagine the pain her kids are feeling. I'm so sad and it's so painful to see how much the kids are hurting. It makes it feel so much better if I can blame the devil and not God for what happened."

This, my friends, is why I am so passionate about what I am writing. I have been in her shoes, seeing bad things happening in my life and thinking that God was allowing it. It made me angry and bitter and tainted my view of God. I think many people are in the same situation—angry or questioning God because they think He had something to do with the bad things that have happened to them. Let me reiterate what the Bible says, "Do not be deceived! God is good and only gives good gifts to us!"

To be continued.

When I heard from my friend about what those two girls went through, it broke my heart. I felt a burning desire to share with them the truth, that God wasn't behind that and didn't want that to happen at all. I wanted to make sure they heard it from someone because I didn't want them to get a wrong impression of God like I had after Matt's accident. I got virtually no feedback on this one, so I was disappointed. Not because I want the praise but because I think it is vital for people to understand this truth. So many people have a warped sense of who God is and what He is really like. Everyone seems to go back to the book of Job, but that was not under our new covenant promises that we have now. I pray that whoever is reading this book truly understands that God does not allow bad things into our lives. The next article expands on this even more.

Jesus Bought Back for Us what Adam and Eve Lost

I heard a story about something that happened to a very well-known man when he was a boy. His family regularly attended church, and when his sister died at a young age, many of those church members came around and told him that God had a reason for allowing it. God must need his sister in heaven.

Because of him hearing those things, this guy became very angry with God. He said if there was a God, he didn't want to have anything to do with Him. This person has become very famous and influential, but because of wrong doctrine being taught, he devoted his life to being against Christians, instead of promoting the kingdom.

Isn't that sad? It is to me. And I see it happening all the time.

One of my friends told me she was watching a popular pastor on TV, and after the Boston Marathon bombings, this pastor made this remark: "Well, God must have a reason for allowing this. Nothing can happen but what He allows." She said she immediately turned him off, and rightfully so! I could not believe that he attributed God to having anything to do with that terrible event. *Tragedy, devastation, evil,* and other like words are used to describe such an awful act of hatred, and then people come along and link God to having something to do with things like that? No way! Why would anyone want to serve a God like that?

Those bombers had a choice. They were inspired by Satan and chose to follow his lies rather than obeying the Holy Spirit, which I'm sure was also speaking to them, telling them not to do it. God is a gentleman, and as much as we would like Him to take over our lives sometimes and make the choices for us and others, He won't overstep the free will He has given to each and every one of us.

I think part of the problem is that most people think that if God wants something done, since He is God, He can just make it happen. But unlike so many people who don't keep their word, God will not violate His Word. Psalm 89:34 states, "My covenant I will not break, nor alter the word that has gone out of My lips."

When God says something, He means it. In Genesis 1:26, God says, "Let Us make man in Our image, according to Our likeness; let them have dominion over the fish of the sea, over the birds of the air, and over the cattle, over all the earth and over every creeping thing that creeps on the earth."

God gave Adam and Eve dominion over the earth, but they sinned and transferred that power over to Satan (Luke 4:6). God couldn't take back that power or He would have violated His Word.

Now do you want to hear the good news? Jesus came as a man and disarmed Satan of his powers on the cross (Colossian 2:15). Jesus gained back this power over the earth that had been lost and has passed it on to us (Matthew 28:18–19). Because He has given us His Spirit, we have exceedingly great power, the same power that raised Jesus from the dead! (Ephesians 1:19–20). We have power over the devil because as 1 John 4:4 states, "He who is in you is greater than he who is in the world." James 4:7 tells us to resist the devil and he will flee from us. If we didn't have power over the devil, then the word of God wouldn't tell us to resist him.

John 14:12 tells us that we are to do the same works that Jesus did, and even greater works than that, because He goes to His Father. Now how are we to do the same works Jesus did, and even greater works than those, if He didn't give us the power to do so? Unfortunately, few people have revelation of this incredible power and responsibility God has given to us. Hosea 4:6 says, "My people are destroyed for lack of knowledge."

To be continued.

This article was never published in the physical paper, only online. There was a mix-up at the paper because the former managing editor had left. I was very disappointed because I really wanted people to read this and understand the authority we have been given as believers. We need to walk in the power that Jesus died to give us. We need to take a stand and prevent some of these tragedies from happening to us and the ones we love.

Melanie wrote, "With all you have been through in your loving family, I am happy to see you understand and believe in God, Amber. Great article!"

Stepping out of my Comfort Zone to Believe the Truth

I remember when the realization hit me that my brother Matt's accident wasn't from God.

It was probably about six or seven years ago after I was learning the truth about God being good and not causing bad things to happen to us and that we have an enemy who seeks to kill, steal, and destroy from us (John 10:10).

One day, it dawned on me that if this all was true, then the beliefs that I had held on to for so long were not true.

Wow, that rocked my world for a moment. Now I had a choice to make. Was I going to believe what I always had because it was comfortable and popular among many believers, or was I going to humble myself, admit I was wrong, and believe the truth? I had believed that God allowed my brother to be killed to bring me and a small handful of others to Christ. I gave my testimony several times, even in the chapel at college. I shared it with the youth group that I had helped with at my local church. I was passionate about what I believed. But I was passionately wrong.

I now knew what was right. I knew I had discovered the real truth about God. Things were making sense like never before, and my view of God changed from an unpredictable Lord who was sometimes loving but other times harsh, to a loving God, my Abba Father, who loves me more than I will ever know. I knew this was the real God I had been searching for.

To all those out there who heard me give my testimony back in the day, I am sorry if I led you astray. I am sorry if I led you to believe that God allows bad things to happen to teach us a lesson. I know my heart was right, but what I was sharing was drastically wrong. God didn't cause or "allow" my brother's death to get me saved, although that is a good thing that He brought out of it. I believe the Holy Spirit was warning Matt to not come home from college that day because He knew what was going to happen. I believe God could have used Matt so much more mightily and reached many more people if he was still here among us. And I believe the enemy knew that.

Let me give you my new testimony: God is good. God wants the best for us, just like any parent wants for their children. I have had many bad things happen to me at my somewhat young age (depends on your definition of young), but God wasn't behind them or allowing them. Satan was. He was stealing, killing, and destroying. But you know what? I now know the truth. I know that I can resist him, and he will flee from me (James 4:6). I wasn't resisting him before because I had blinders on. I thought God controlled everything, and when you have that mentality, you won't be resisting the devil because you will think you are resisting God. I know that greater is He who is in me, than he (Satan) who is in the world (1 John 4:4). Since I have discovered the truth, I am going to use all that is within me to proclaim the goodness of God. What the enemy meant to destroy me, I am going to use against him. It is my life's mission to share with others what I have learned and to teach them the truth, that God is a good God! Oh, how freeing the truth is. Oh, how good God is!

Abby wrote, "Great article! Hope lots of people read this!"

Krystal wrote, "People's testimony changes. I don't believe you led anyone down the wrong path. You spoke from where you were spiritually at that time. You have grown as a Christian and a child of God—that is the true testimony."

Heather wrote, "Wow, you hit the nail on the head! Great article…thanks for sharing."

This was written straight from my heart. This is what I want people to hear. God is so good! People seemed receptive to it, so I was very thankful for that. I have to admit, I got a little paranoid after these last few articles came out because some people have adamant feelings against these truths. I have been persecuted in the past for saying that God didn't want, cause, or allow bad things to happen in people's lives. I thought it would bring them freedom like it did for me, but I guess they took comfort in having a warped sense of God. I pray for the truth of God and His goodness to manifest in the hearts and minds of believers everywhere!

Encouragement Is a Chance to Be Used as a Blessing from God

I woke up early this morning really needing my time alone with God to renew my mind and get refocused.

This had been a hard week for me. The boys had been extra rowdy and active, and my discipline efforts seemed to be to no avail. This had led me to be physically, emotionally, and spiritually fatigued.

I was looking forward to getting recharged this morning, but the boys were all up by 6:30 a.m., which put a big dent in my plans. I was discouraged and praying for someone to just show up out of the blue to help me out for a bit.

Then something happened that completely changed my day. A card came for me in the mail. The front of the card read: "Motherhood is not for wimps." On the inside it said, "You're making a difference EVERY DAY!"

It was from my friend Erin. As I read her kind words, I broke out in tears. She said she realized how hard a stage I am in right now, but my choice to stay at home is making a difference in the lives of both my children and my husband. She encouraged me to keep pressing forward.

Wow, what a difference that made in me. What rejuvenation! It pumped such life into my tired, weary body and reminded me of my incredible purpose in life right now to raise my boys up right. I just started thanking God for using Erin to encourage me, thanking Him for her friendship and praising Him for caring so much about me that He prompted her to send me that card.

Never underestimate what a little encouragement can do for someone. It is a way to be used by God to be a blessing to someone in need, and that is exciting! I believe God speaks to us all the time through the Holy Spirit, telling us ways we can meet someone's need. Sad thing is, some people are too busy to hear the Holy Spirit, and others listen but don't act. *A lot of people have good intentions, but it's the people that follow through on them that make a difference. It wouldn't have helped me if Erin had just thought about sending a card. What helped me was that she actually did it!*

It doesn't take a special talent or vast resources to be a blessing. Make a meal for someone, stop in for a visit, or just give them a call to see how they are doing. Pay someone a compliment if the thought comes to you. Many people have said kind words to me about my articles, and that has truly encouraged and blessed me. (If you have done so, thank you!)

James 4:17 says, "Therefore, to him who knows to do good and does not do it, to him it is sin." God isn't mad at us if we don't do what we know we should do, but it is sin. We are missing out on an incredible opportunity to be a blessing to someone in need.

I want to encourage you to follow through on what the Holy Spirit leads you to do, even if it seems weird. People could be praying for something very specific, and you could be God's chosen vessel to answer that prayer.

Have I missed opportunities to do this? Yes, as I know everyone has. But I believe my misses are becoming fewer as I seek the Lord passionately, desiring to be used by Him. I'll let you in on a secret: being a blessing and helping others blesses you as well!

Ask the Holy Spirit to lead you, be still enough so you can hear Him, and be excited that you can be a difference maker. Never miss the opportunity to be a blessing and source of encouragement to someone. You never know what kind of impact it may make not only on their life but on yours as well.

Motherhood has been an inexpressible joy but also tremendous work. AJ and Grady were just three and two when Braxton was born. It was very crazy (and still is) in our house. I would pray all the time for people to have compassion and stop in to help, visit, or just ask how I was doing. My prayers seemed unanswered, but God has shown me that He answered as soon as I prayed. The problem was that He had to use people to get my prayers accomplished, and like I had mentioned, people were either too busy to hear Him or just didn't obey. I want to make sure that I never get too busy to hear God speaking to me and showing me ways I can help others. I was very thankful that my friend Erin made herself available to hear God speaking to her as well.

Don't Push Away God's Love; Allow Yourself to Be Loved by Him

Ever since I became a mom, one of my favorite things has been to snuggle up with one of my little guys and rock them to sleep. Those times are dwindling though as AJ and Grady are both too big for that now and Braxton is quickly growing up before my eyes. But once in a while, I still get a chance to rock Braxton. I love when that little guy rests his head against my shoulder and relaxes in my arms. Those are special moments that I cherish.

During those precious times alone with my son, I always end up thanking God for him and thinking about how much I love him. Tears would form in my eyes because of the love that abounds in my heart for him. But then a realization hit me. As much as I love him, God loves him even more. And as I ran my fingers through his soft, strawberry-blond hair, I remember that God takes such an interest in him that He even knows the number of hairs on his head! (Matthew 10:30, Luke 12:7). Isn't that amazing to think about?

Then a thought came to me, which I believe was Holy Spirit–inspired, reminding me that God loves me as much as He loves Braxton and knows the amount of hairs on my head as well! (And yours too!)

When I think about it that way, it puts a different twist on things. Sure, it is easy for me to picture God seeing my precious little boy in that way, but it doesn't come quite as easily to picture God seeing me in the same manner.

Why is that? Why is it easy for us to tell others that God loves them but it isn't always as easy for us to tell ourselves the same thing? Maybe it is because we know our own unworthiness. We know we haven't done everything right and don't deserve such love being poured out toward us. But aren't you glad God doesn't love us based on our actions and worthiness? I sure am!

The disciple John had a wonderful grasp of the love that Jesus had for him. In the gospel of John that he wrote, he referred to himself five times as the disciple that Jesus loved (John 12:23, 19:26, 20:2, 21:7, and 21:20).

In today's world, many people would be critical of someone who referred to themselves like John did. People would make comments such as, "What makes you so special?" or "Do you think you are better than everyone else?" Popular opinion would be to call that person proud and arrogant.

We all should have the same mind-set as John. I think a great lesson to learn from John is that he allowed himself to be loved by Jesus. Many people resist the love of Christ because of what I mentioned before; they feel unworthy. But John didn't push Jesus away; he embraced Him.

I don't think John had a "God loves me because I'm so great" type of attitude, but rather a "God loves me because *He's* so great" attitude. I don't believe Jesus loved John more than the others, and I don't think John thought that either. I believe that John referred to himself in that way as a reminder to himself of the love Jesus had for him and to serve as a model for us as well.

I challenge you to begin thinking, believing, and saying out loud to yourself that you are the disciple whom Jesus loved. Let that sink into your entire being. This is not arrogance. It is how God feels about you, and arrogance is thinking you know more than God!

"We love Him because He first loved us" (1 John 4:19). If we can comprehend what is the width and length and depth and height (Ephesians 3:19) of the love of our Father toward us, our hearts would overflow with such love and gratitude that we would never want to stop praising and thanking God, and I can guarantee we would never be the same again.

This was one of my favorite articles because I love to write about how much God loves us. People need to know this! Lives would be changed if we would get a comprehension of God's amazing love for us all.

A reader named Carrie wrote, "Can I just say once again how much I love to read your articles. Why don't you compile them for a daily devotional book? I would buy it! Thanks for the reminder of His great love for us!"

Well, Carrie, thank you, and I hope you follow through on your promise to buy one!

Discovering Another Amazing Truth about Our Wonderful God

How do you view God? This is not a rhetorical question. I really want you to think about it. Whether you have ever consciously thought about it or not, everyone has formed a mental image of who they think God is and what He is like.

I believe far too many people see God as angry and harsh. But that is not so. God is not mad at us; He is loving and kind toward us. He loves us more than we will ever know and so much more than we deserve. Jesus has reconciled us to God through His sacrifice, and God is not mad anymore! Let me show you with scripture.

> "With a little wrath I hid My face from you for a moment; But with everlasting kindness I will have mercy on you," says the Lord, your Redeemer. "For this is like the waters of Noah to Me; For as I have sworn that the waters of Noah would no longer cover the earth, So have I sworn that I would not be angry with you, nor rebuke you. For the mountains shall depart and the hills be removed, but My kindness shall not depart from you, nor shall My covenant of peace be removed," says the Lord, who has mercy on you. (Isaiah 54:8–10)

This first verse is referring back to Deuteronomy 31:17, which was under the old covenant. God was mad at the people of Israel because they were worshipping other gods and broke the covenant He had made with them. But we are now under the new covenant of grace through the blood of

Jesus, and the rest of these verses are prophesying how God would be treating us under this new covenant. (The previous chapter, Isaiah 53, prophesies of the coming Messiah.)

Most people don't even realize there is a difference between the old covenant and the new covenant. This is why many people view God as mean and harsh, because they look at how things happened under the old covenant of law (I will explain this all in more detail in a future article), and they don't realize we are now under the new covenant of grace. There is a huge difference.

It goes on to say that God will always be kind to us and He will not be mad at us. Wow, are you getting this? Do you see a difference? These are the words of God to us, and it is impossible for God to lie (Hebrews 6:18). How can this be, that God will not be mad at us, that His kindness shall not depart from us, and His covenant of peace will never be removed from us? One word answer: Jesus!

Isaiah 53:10–11 says, "Yet it pleased the Lord to bruise Him; He has put Him to grief…He shall see the labor of His soul, and be satisfied…By His knowledge My righteous Servant shall justify many, For He shall bear their iniquities."

This says it pleased the Lord to bruise Jesus. How could it please a loving Father to see His Son suffer? Because God knew the one-time sacrifice of Jesus was paying the price for the sins of the entire world. It made God happy to know that now man would be reconciled to Himself through Jesus (2 Corinthians 5:18–19). Sin, which had caused a rift in the relationship, was paid for on the body of Jesus. Hallelujah! Thank you, Jesus!

I understand this may be hard for some to swallow because God has probably been misrepresented to you as being angry and harsh, yet He is just the opposite. He is always kind to us, will never be mad at us, and will always have mercy on us. Realizing those incredible truths has taken my relationship with God to a completely different level. And I pray it will do the same for you.

I encourage you start meditating on these verses and pray for the Holy Spirit to enlighten you. Then start praising God for His love, kindness, and incredible gift of Jesus to us today!

Melanie wrote, "So well put. Thank you, Amber. God has truly blessed you with a wonderful gift. It's wonderful how you're using that gift to reach others."

Thank you, Lord for this amazing platform You have given to me. I love writing about how good You are! Those verses in Isaiah should just blow away the wrong concept that so many people have of You. You are good and You are not mad at us because our sin has been paid for on the body of Your Son. You love us, and You are not punishing us because You already punished Jesus. Halleluiah!

All Sin Has Been Paid for on the Body of Jesus

In my last article, I wrote about how God is not mad at us. I want to share something else that is closely related to God not being mad at us, and it is the fact that God is not punishing us for our sins anymore.

I know this goes against most people's view of God. Many people see God as sitting up there in heaven, just waiting for us to sin so He can punish us. But that is not so. God will always have mercy on us (Isaiah 54:8, 10).

A simple definition of mercy is God not giving us what we deserve. We deserve to be punished for our sins, but because of Jesus, He will never give us what we deserve. There is only one sin that anyone will get punished for, and that is the sin of rejecting Jesus as their Savior (John 3:17–18).

King David lived under the law in a time when He was being punished for His sins. He longed to live in the age of grace we are now in. Romans 4:7–8 quotes David prophesying about the future, in which he says, "Blessed are those whose lawless deeds are forgiven, and whose sins are covered; Blessed is the man to whom the Lord shall not impute sin." David's desire is our reality. What powerful and amazing scriptures. The Lord is not imputing sin to us anymore. Impute means that He is not holding it against us, or charging it to our account. God is not charging sin to our account anymore.

Second Corinthians 5:19 states, "That God was in Christ, reconciling the world to Himself, not imputing their trespasses to them, and has committed to us the word of reconciliation." We need to be sharing this good news. Because of Jesus, we have been reconciled to God, and we are no longer being punished for our sins.

Jeremiah prophesied about Jesus and the new covenant of grace. Hebrews 8:8,12–13 says, "Behold the days are coming, says the Lord, when I will make a new covenant with the house of Israel and the house of Judah…For I will be merciful to their unrighteousness, and their sins and their lawless deeds I will remember no more." In that He says "a new covenant," He has made the first obsolete.

This is the good news of the new covenant we are now in.

Romans 6:15 says we are not under law but under grace, and Romans 5:13 states that sin is not imputed when there is no law. Like I mentioned before, under the law, they were punished for their sins. The first person to violate the Ten Commandments picked up sticks on the Sabbath and God told them to stone him (Numbers 15:32–36). God is not dealing with us like that anymore.

If God were to punish us now for our sins, He would be saying that the sacrifice of Jesus wasn't enough. All that physical, spiritual, and emotional pain He went through for us didn't quite take care of all the sin. That just isn't so. Jesus died once for *all* sins. God would be unjust to judge us for sins He already judged in Jesus.

Romans 6:9–10 reads, "Knowing that Christ, having been raised from the dead, dies no more. Death no longer has dominion over Him. For the death that He died, He died to sin once for all." Hebrews 10:10,12 says, "By that will we have been sanctified through the offering of the body of Jesus Christ once for all…But this man, after He had offered one sacrifice for sins forever, sat down at the right hand of God."

Jesus was offered one time for all. He wasn't just offered as a sacrifice for your sins up until you were born again. He died two thousand years ago, and Jesus isn't being sacrificed again every time we sin. Unlike the old covenant where the high priest had to enter the most holy place every year to make atonement for sins, Jesus made atonement once for us all (Hebrews 9:25–28).

What incredibly good news this is! Can you see why I am passionate about Jesus? What an amazing God we serve, who is so rich in grace and mercy.

I encourage you to study these scriptures yourself. Pray for the spirit of wisdom and revelation to be upon you in the knowledge of Him (Ephesians 1:17). How great is our Father's love for us all. How great is the sacrifice of Jesus!

What awesome news that Jesus has paid for all our sins! People need to catch hold of that revelation and truth!

One lady told me that she reread this article several times and used information from it to share with kids she was teaching at her church. Boy, that hit me. Lord, what influence You have given me. Keep using me to teach Your children about the incredible sacrifice of Your Son!

We Are More than Conquerors through Him Who Loved Us

I take this column very seriously. It is my ministry, my chance to be Christ's ambassador, to share His love and grace with a world that desperately needs it. I have many topics I want to write about, and sometimes I wonder if I will be able to share them in a way that is understandable yet powerfully conveys the truth. I do try hard to rest in the Lord and allow Him to speak through me because I know on my own I can't do this.

Today I was putting pressure on myself because of a major topic I want to write about. I was feeling inadequate for the task at hand. I had faith that God would speak to me but not faith in myself to hear Him. I had a lot of doubt in myself. I even said aloud one time, "God, I know You want me to get the word out more than I do. I just don't know if I will be able to say it right." Then the Holy Spirit started bringing scripture to my mind. He reminded me of Romans 8:37, which says, "Yet in all these things we are more than conquerors through Him who loved us."

I started meditating on that verse, and faith rose up on the inside of me. I began wondering why I was acting so defeated when I had the one who conquered death living on the inside of me. I realized I was looking at myself and my abilities, instead of who is in me and *His* abilities. I am more than a conqueror through Christ.

I remember about a year ago when this verse really came alive to me. I had read it several times before, but that morning while reading my Bible, I saw it differently. It hit me that these were not just mere words; this was truth, the inspired Word of God. I looked up the meaning of *conqueror*—"a person who conquerors or vanquishes; victor." Wow, I am more than a victor through Christ! How powerful!

It would have been incredible enough if it had just said we were conquerors or victors. But to emphasize this incredible power that is in every born-again believer, it says we are more than conquerors! Can't you just hear God speaking through this verse to every believer, saying, "Don't limit what I am able to do through you. Don't have a defeated attitude. Don't look to yourself and your own abilities, but look to Me and My incredible power. Through Me, you are not just the victor, but you are even more than that. I am able to do exceedingly, abundantly, beyond all you ask or imagine according to my power at work within you" (Ephesians 3:20).

I can't stress how important it is to renew our minds to the incredible truths that the Word of God says about us. Just meditating on those two verses caused a complete transformation in my attitude. Romans 12:2 says that renewing our mind will transform us, and that is so very true. I went from fear to confidence. From relying on my own strength to relying on the One who gives me strength, the One that I can do all things through. Instead of looking at myself in the natural, I started seeing myself in the spirit. I now have the spirit of Jesus living inside of me (Galatians 4:6). I have the mind of Christ in my spirit (1 Corinthians 2:16), and as Jesus is, so am I in this world (1 John 4:17).

I want to encourage you to start seeing yourself as the conqueror, not the conquered; the victor, not the victim. Meditate on these scriptures until they become as real to you as they did to me. Know that you have the Spirit of the Living God inside of you, and nothing is impossible.

※

A reader named Mark wrote, "Very encouraging word, Amber. Thanks for such an on-time message."

The day this verse originally came alive to me (we are more than conquerors through Christ) was very timely. That evening, I was heavily persecuted by someone close to me because I was telling his wife that God didn't want or allow the bad things that were happening in her life. He tried to discredit me on the phone, and it left me very hurt, but not crushed. I kept meditating on that verse that I was more than a conqueror, and although the enemy was trying to knock me down, he wasn't going to win.

Shall We Continue in Sin that Grace May Abound?

In my writings, I try to stress the love, grace, and goodness of God because not only is it the truth, but I know it is what truly changes people. It is what truly changed me.

If you read two of my previous articles about God not being mad at us and not punishing us for our sins, it may lead you to ask the question: does that mean we can just go and live however we want since we are now under grace?

Paul, the apostle of grace, addressed this question three different times in the book of Romans (Romans 3:8, 6:1, and 6:15). And I would respond the same way that Paul did: certainly not! How shall we who died to sin live any longer in it? (Romans 6:2).

Sin is stupid. There are many reasons why we shouldn't sin. Our nature has changed, it gives place to the devil, it hurts our witness, and most of all, it goes against God and takes the sacrifice of Jesus in vain. There are consequences to sin although it is not God who is causing those consequences.

Holy living is important. I am adamantly opposed to sin. But here is where the paradigm shift has occurred in me: understanding how much God loves me through His free gift of Jesus is now my motivator for right living. When you know how much someone loves you, especially when you least deserve it, the last thing you want to do is go against them.

Let's say one night my husband brought home flowers for no reason, cooked supper for me and the kids, and then told me that I had the night off to go and relax and do whatever I want. How do you think I would respond to that? Would that make me want to go and do something to hurt him? Of course not! That would encourage me to be the best wife I could be.

It is the same with God. Knowing that He is not angry with me or going to punish me when I mess up does not make me want to go out and live in sin. Just the opposite! It causes me to devote my entire being to living for His glory and magnifying His holy name. Right living then comes as a byproduct of right believing in His goodness and amazing love.

My relationship with God used to be love mixed with fear. I did love God and didn't want to go against Him, but there was also a fear factor involved. Fear of what God would do to me if I did mess up. Fear of His wrath and punishment. I was always thinking of myself and what I had to do. I lived in a world of self-righteousness and condemnation. Let me tell you, that was bondage.

Fear involves torment, but perfect love casts out fear (1 John 4:18). When we are constantly looking at ourselves and what we have to do, we aren't looking at Jesus and what He actually did. We very rarely feel peace. Well, how can we when our eyes are always on ourselves? The scripture tells us the way to peace is by keeping our eyes on Jesus (Isaiah 26:3).

Love is such a better motivator than fear. *Fear can restrain behavior, but it does not change hearts.* Love is what changes hearts. When you get the revelation of how much God loves you, your actions will automatically follow. You will end up serving Him better out of love than you ever did out of fear.

This is what has happened to me. My living holy (and no, I am not saying I am perfect) is now the fruit of my relationship with God, not the root to a relationship with God, and it is all because of what Jesus has done for me. Thanks be to God for His indescribable gift!

My eyes have been opened to the fact that my actions could never be enough. I can never earn the favor of God or do anything to deserve it; it is given freely to me because of Jesus and His grace. There is such freedom in trusting in His goodness rather than trusting in my own goodness. I pray you will get revelation of this and experience that love and freedom as well.

Oh what a difference this truth has made in my life, and I want it to change others lives as well! If you have never received God's love and have always been motivated by fear, you can't see how it can work. I have had someone accuse me of promoting sin. That is actually a twisted compliment because it puts me in the same category as Paul, the preacher of grace. Once people truly understand grace, they all agree that they are motivated not to sin out of love, not fear. One of my friends shared with me that he had an addiction to tobacco for nine years. He wanted to quit but just couldn't. But when he started understanding grace, it allowed him to break free from the bondage of the addiction. Grace doesn't promote sin; it frees us from sin!

An Animal's Love May Be Conditional, but God's Love Is Unconditional

Currently at our house, we have five kittens and one cat, all kept outdoors to help minimize the mice and mole population. Most of them are wild and won't let us get close enough to pet them. The mother of all but one kitten is named Calli. She has been coming around more lately, and when she sees me coming with food, she doesn't run off as quickly as she once did.

For some strange reason, I really want that cat to like me. I find myself looking forward to having table scraps so I can take them outside and give them to her, hoping she will come and realize that I am her friend, not her enemy. It has worked to some degree, and occasionally, she lets me pet her while eating.

One night, Calli saw me and came running. But this time, I didn't have any food. When she realized that, she had no interest in me. She didn't want to be around me because she liked me; she wanted to be around me because of what I could give her. And when I wasn't giving her anything, she didn't have any use for me. I tried to get her to come so I could pet her, but she wouldn't. My husband made the comment, "Amber, her love for you is conditional." And right, he was.

That stuck in my mind. It made me think of how God's love is just the opposite. Whereas Calli's love for me was conditional, based on what I could do for her, God's love is unconditional, not based on what we do for Him.

I don't think enough people have a revelation of this amazing love of God. I know I used to say that God loved me, but it wasn't a revelation deep down in my heart. And most of the time, I based God's love for me on how deserving I thought I was to receive it. It wasn't until I started seeing how good God is and His amazing grace that this love of God became real to me.

I know now that God's love for me is not based on me and my goodness. It is based on my Savior Jesus and His goodness. When I mess up, it doesn't make God love me any less, just like doing good doesn't make Him love me any more. Wow, such a burden has been lifted off my shoulders, and the love of my Savior has flooded my soul!

> Who shall separate us from the love of Christ? Shall tribulation, or distress, or persecution, or famine, or nakedness, or peril, or sword? For I am persuaded that neither death nor life, nor angels nor principalities nor powers, nor things present nor things to come, nor height nor depth, nor any other created thing, shall be able to separate us from the love of God which is in Christ Jesus our Lord. (Romans 8:35, 38–39)

Despite every circumstance we may come across, God is constantly pouring out His love to us. God is not the problem. We are the problem. Most people separate themselves from God's love by not receiving it.

I believe others feel like I used to. When I was "good," then I was worthy of God's love; but when I "messed up," I wasn't. This is not a doctrine of God but a doctrine of the enemy who wants to keep us from experiencing the overwhelming love of God. He knows when we grasp this incredible love of God, we will become world overcomers. Nothing will be able to stop us because after all, if God is for us, who can be against us? (Romans 8:31). The enemy is scared of that, so he constantly tries to make us think we are unworthy of God's love. Revelations 12:10 calls him the "accuser of our brethren."

Don't fall for his trap. Jesus died to make you worthy. Stop looking at yourself and whether you think you deserve God's love. None of us deserve it, but praise Jesus that because of Him, we are getting this amazing love that we don't deserve.

Don't take this sacrifice of Jesus in vain; receive His love for you today.

Oh that dumb cat. Why I wanted it to like me was beyond me. Yet I think it is human nature to want to be loved, even if it is by an animal. I am so thankful I can never be separated from God's love. What an amazing God we serve!

Every Day Should Be Thanksgiving for the Believer

I'm very grateful to Abraham Lincoln for establishing Thanksgiving, a day when we reflect on all the things we have to be thankful for. I'm not trying to discount Thanksgiving, but I believe we, especially those who are followers of Jesus, should make this attitude of thankfulness a way of life, not just practice it during a holiday season. We should live with an "attitude of gratitude."

Having a thankful attitude is so important. Thankfulness softens your heart; it makes you appreciate what you have, appreciate God, and appreciate others more.

Have you ever noticed that people who are the grouchiest and unhappiest are generally the ones that are the least grateful? Picture in your mind someone you know who never seems happy, and I think you will agree. Some people come to my mind, and they definitely aren't ones who make a habit of being thankful. Rather, they have a habit of complaining and focusing on all the negative things in their lives.

A thankful heart leads to contentment while an ungrateful heart leads to discontentment. Romans 1:21 says, "[B]ecause, although they knew God, they did not glorify Him as God, nor were thankful, but became futile in their thoughts, and their foolish hearts were darkened."

An ungrateful heart leads to a hardened heart toward God. In essence, you are saying, "God, you haven't done enough for me." This leads to an underlying bitterness toward God for all the things that are wrong. But a thankful heart keeps you sensitive toward God.

Since I have learned more about the grace of God and what this really means, my thankfulness level has increased dramatically, and that is what scriptures tells us will happen. Second Corinthians 4:15 says, "For all things are for your sakes, that grace, having spread through the many, may cause thanksgiving to abound to the glory of God."

When the gospel of grace (unmerited favor) is taught and received, it causes hearts to abound in gratefulness toward God.

I can verify that in my own life. I used to think when I did good, God "owed me," that I deserved a blessing from Him through my good works. I sure didn't understand that grace is His unearned, unmerited favor toward me and that my actions could never even put a dent in the debt that Jesus paid for me. Since my eyes have been opened to the fact that God doesn't owe me anything but He freely gives to me anyway because He loves me, it causes thanksgiving and gratefulness to flow freely from me toward God. I don't have to force myself to thank God. I rejoice that I get to thank God. What a privilege I have to thank my wonderful God for all the incredible things He has done for me at the expense of His innocent Son.

We really try to stress to our sons the importance of having a thankful attitude. We want them to truly be thankful and not have an entitlement attitude that is so prevalent today. The other day I was busy doing something, and AJ wanted to play go fish. No one else wanted to play, so I dropped what I was doing and told him I would play with him. That little boy ran up, hugged me, and said, "Oh, thank you, Mommy! Thank you so much!" His reaction really blessed me. Think about how much it must bless God when we thank Him.

I want to encourage and challenge you to live with an attitude of gratitude. Ephesians 5:20 says, "Giving thanks always for all things to God the Father in the name of our Lord Jesus Christ." Thank God for everything He has done for you. Not just the big things, but the small things as well. A hot shower, clothes to wear, a place to sleep. These things may seem insignificant, but I can guarantee when you start thanking God for them, you will not only appreciate them much more but will also find yourself growing closer to God in the process.

What a difference having a thankful heart has made for me. The days I am thankful are good days, but the days I start thinking about what is wrong and am not being thankful are my grouchy days! We all have so much to be thankful for, and having a thankful attitude can bring the light of Christ into any room. I believe (although I know people disagree with this) that thankfulness can bring us out of depression because it has us thinking on all that is right instead of wrong. Thankfulness is so very important, and we should all make it a continual habit.

One of the Most Valuable Pieces of Advice I Have Ever Received

A friend of mine has recently started seeking God, which was so exciting to hear. She said she started reading a few chapters of her Bible a night although she didn't understand very much of it.

I told her to read the New Testament first. Then I gave her one of the most valuable pieces of advice I have ever received. I told her whenever she does read the Old Testament, she needs to read it in light of the finished work of Jesus on the cross. This may not sound like such an important truth, but it really is. It has helped me to understand the Bible so much more and put things in proper perspective.

Second Corinthians 3:12–16 says, "Therefore, since we have such hope, we use great boldness of speech, unlike Moses, who put a veil over his face so that the children of Israel could not look steadily at the end of what was passing away. But their minds were blinded. For until this day the same veil remains unlifted in the reading of the Old Testament, because the veil is taken away in Christ. But even to this day, when Moses is read, a veil lies on the heart. Nevertheless, when one turns to the Lord, the veil is taken away."

All the verses leading up to these are talking about the Old Testament law. "When Moses is read" refers to the Ten Commandments and all the other laws that go along with it. That was under the old covenant, but we now have a new covenant of grace through the blood of Jesus. "The law was given through Moses, but grace and truth came through Jesus Christ" (John 1:17).

If you just read through the Old Testament, without being mindful of the new covenant, your mind is blinded to what Jesus has already accomplished. The Old Testament is not wrong; all scripture is given by inspiration of God (2 Timothy 3:16), but we need to rightly divide the word of truth (2 Timothy 2:15). When we don't read the Old Testament in retrospect of what Jesus has already done, our minds are blinded to the goodness and grace of God. The word of truth is the word of God, but we need to accurately interpret it based on the work of Jesus on the cross. Then, when we know Jesus and His sacrifice, the veil, spiritual blindness from the law, is taken away, and we can properly see the goodness of God.

Let me provide some examples. Deuteronomy 28 shares all the blessings and curses of the law. If you followed the law perfectly, you would be blessed; but if you didn't follow the law, you would be cursed. This sounds scary, but this is where knowing what Jesus did on the cross takes out all the fear and reveals the truth.

Galatians 3:13 says, "Christ has redeemed us from the curse of the law, having become a curse for us (for it is written, 'Cursed is everyone who hangs on a tree')." Jesus became a curse for us on the cross so we can freely through grace receive the blessings of God. He fulfilled the righteous requirement of the law for us (Romans 8:3–4).

Another example would be Psalms 51:11–12, which says, "Create in me a clean heart, O God, and renew a steadfast spirit within me. Do not cast me away from Your presence, and do not take Your Holy Spirit from me."

Those things were okay for David to pray because he didn't have the covenant we now have. He couldn't be born again at that point because Jesus hadn't yet died and risen again. He didn't have the Holy Spirit residing in him at all times like we do, and his heart and his spirit couldn't be cleansed. But if we are born again, our spirits are cleansed, the Holy Spirit is always with us, and God will never leave us or forsake us (1 John 3:24, 1 John 4:13, John 14:6, Hebrews 13:5). We actually have the spirit of Jesus living in us, so obviously, our spirits are as clean as they can get.

The Bible does not contradict itself, but there is a difference between the old and new covenant. Understanding this has really helped tie it all together for me. Now when I read the Old Testament and understand what I have been delivered from, it makes me appreciate the sacrifice of Jesus so much more.

People seemed very receptive to this, and I was so thankful for that. Knowing this has really helped me tremendously. Many things that I couldn't understand in the Old Testament have become clearer after learning this truth, and I want others to know that as well. We need to rightly divide the word of truth!

Solving the Mystery of Grandma Lucy's Hope Chest

This morning, I was going through items in the house, and I came upon a small hope chest that had belonged to my grandma Lucy. I remember my uncle Jim calling me a few years back, telling me he had something of grandma's that she wanted me to have. She had written on a piece of paper and taped it firmly to the bottom of the chest: For Amber Rice.

I had wondered why Grandma specifically wanted me to have it. We were very close, and I went to visit her often, but there were papers in that chest pertaining to her first husband, Chap, who was not my grandfather. So I was a little perplexed as to why she was so adamant that I have it.

This morning, I looked through it again. A small picture button of Grandma, circa 1910, both her and Chap's confirmation books, and their marriage license were just a few of the valuable treasures in it. Then I ran across a letter, one that I hadn't noticed before.

The letter was typed and dated March 28, 1931. It was written by a friend or relative who had heard that my grandma had a stillborn child. It obviously meant a lot to her to have saved it. Here is a quote from the letter:

> I hope that you will understand that it is an All-wise power, beyond all human understanding, that creates and also takes away and that it was His will, and sometime you will fully understand just why it had to be.

This person meant well, but they were misinformed. As I read the letter, I started crying. Crying for the pain that my grandma must have felt. Crying because she thought God was behind it all. And worse yet, just a few years later, her husband Chap died, and Grandma was left alone to raise two young children. I am sure she received more letters saying God was behind that too. I thought about how she lived her whole life believing that God allowed all that pain and suffering, not knowing that things happen out of the will of God and we have an enemy who seeks to steal, kill, and destroy. Tears rolled as I looked back on her life because she never got to truly understand the complete goodness of God. She was saved and did love God, but always, in the back of her mind had to be the resonating question, "Why, God?"

I believe that was one of the first things that my grandma may have asked God when she got to heaven: "Why did you take my child and young husband?" And I believe God's answer would have been something like this:

> My precious Lucy, I was not behind the death of your baby or husband. Why would I create and form this child in your womb and then take her from you? Why would I bless you with this husband and father to your children and then take him from you and leave you a widow and your children fatherless? I only give good gifts (James 1:16–17). I wept to see you in such pain. My child, those things happened out of my will. The devil has blinded many people to the truth about Me from the beginning in the garden. He is the author of tragedy and then convinces people that I am behind it so he can keep them from knowing the truth about Me.

And I think when grandma would hear God's answer, she would have cried tears of remorse. I picture her saying, "I wish someone would have told me this when I was still alive so I wouldn't have had to live with that nagging question my whole life. I wish I would have known how truly good You were while I was still on earth!"

I believe I now know why my grandma wanted me to have that chest. The Holy Spirit told her to give it to me. God knew I would read that eighty-two-year-old letter and be moved to share His goodness and truth through the platform He has given to me.

Maybe you are going through pain and you think God caused it. Please know that God is good, He only gives good gifts, and things may happen out of His will. I want everyone to learn that truth now, so people can understand the love and goodness of God while still on earth. If I would have known what I know now when my grandma was still alive, I would have shared it with her. I can't share with her anymore, but I can share with all of you.

This article is dear to my heart. I remember the day clearly; my mom had watched the boys that morning so I could clean up and start packing because we were going to be moving. As I read that letter, the tears just flowed and flowed. I felt so bad for my grandma Lucy. Oh how I loved that lady! And to know that she lived out her life thinking God had caused those tragedies broke my heart. I can't imagine the incredible pain she felt and how often she asked God that question of why.

Grandma Lucy was well-known around our community, and most people referred to her as "Grandma Lucy" as well. She was a very short, pear-shaped lady with an outgoing spirit and friendly demeanor. She could be seen driving through town (very slowly, I might add) with her fluorescent yellowish/greenish Ford Maverick. I have yet to see another car that color in my entire life. Everybody knew that was Grandma Lucy coming.

I believe this article touched a lot of people because they knew her, and I received a lot of feedback on it.

One reader named Gina wrote, "Thank you, Amber! I struggle a lot with this, and I know I was supposed to read this particular article. I remember Lucy and think of baseball and her yellow car packed with kids! After I was married, she showed a bunch of pictures of wedding cakes she had made. We had lived at the apartments at the same time. How lucky to have a wonderful person that you carry with you!"

Another reader named Molly wrote, "So beautifully written and true. The enemy throws those veils out there to dishearten us and try to distance many from God. Your words and story will enlighten many."

Praise God that some people are getting this. Religion has sucked so many people into believing that everything that happens is God's will, and that is not so. I know it gave me a false representation of who God is and what He is like. God only wants good things for us!

Lord, I pray for more and more opportunities to share about Your goodness and love with so many people that need to hear it.

When the Fullness of the Time Had Come, God Sent Forth His Son

Have you ever wondered why it took God so long to send Jesus to earth as our Savior? Maybe it is something you have never thought about, but I think a lot of people have.

God's timing is perfect, even if we don't always understand it. I believe if God would have sent Jesus sooner, the people wouldn't have been ready to receive Him. Let me explain.

Let's look at the people of Israel when they were brought out of Egypt. God performed miracles and brought them all out safely. But what kind of attitudes did they have? Were they thankful? Absolutely not. They were always grumbling and didn't honor and reverence God the way they should have. What if God would have brought Jesus to them then? They wouldn't have seen their need for Him. So what did God do instead? He gave the law.

In Exodus 19, God was testing their hearts. God was telling Moses that if they obey His voice and keep His covenant, they would be a treasure to Him (Exodus 19:5). I believe this is talking about the covenant He made with Abraham, which was based on faith, and was before the law was given (Romans 4:3, 5, 13).

Exodus 19:8 has their reply to God: "Then all the people answered together and said, 'All that the Lord has spoken we will do.'" Now this reply doesn't really seem wrong, but

I have heard a teaching from someone who is very fluent in Hebrew and Greek, and he said in the original Hebrew, it has a much different, deeper meaning. They said it in a very proud way, more like, "Sure, God, whatever you give us we can do. No big deal." In essence, they were saying that they just wanted God to give them a few rules and then leave them alone. They didn't really need God all that much. They were a very proud people. But rules and laws don't take faith. God is looking for faith.

So right after they gave their response to God, what happened? He gave them the law. Before the law, God was primarily dealing with the human race in mercy. Sin is not imputed when there is no law (Romans 5:13). But after the law was given, that all changed. Three thousand were killed after the law was given because they made the golden calf (Exodus 32:28). God was not dealing with them in mercy anymore but rather based on their performance. Romans 4:15 says, "Because the law brings about wrath; for where there is no law there is no transgression." The law brought about the wrath of God.

So why would God do this? Why did God give the law? It wasn't because God is a mean God; it was given to make the people see how they could never be good enough on their own and that they needed a Savior. Galatians 3:19, 23–25 reads, "What purpose then does the law serve? It was added because of transgressions, till the Seed should come to whom the promise was made; and it was appointed through angels by the hand of a mediator [Moses]. But before faith came, we were kept under guard by the law, kept for the faith which would afterward be revealed. Therefore the law was our tutor to bring us to Christ, that we might be justified by faith. But after faith has come, we are no longer under a tutor."

Those are incredible verses. God gave the law to make people see that they weren't as good as what they thought and they could never be good enough; it pointed them to their need for Jesus. When the time was just right, when they were most ready to receive, God sent His Son.

Galatians 4:4–5 says, "But when the fullness of the time had come, God sent forth His Son, born of a woman, born under the law, to redeem those who were under the law, that we might receive the adoption as sons."

Through faith in Jesus as our Savior, we are redeemed from the law. We are no longer judged by God based on our performance. We are accepted because of Jesus and adopted into the family of God! We are no longer a slave to the law but are heirs of God through Christ (Galatians 4:7).

What incredibly good news. I encourage you to read these verses for yourselves and take time to thank God for His gift of Jesus to us all!

Thank You, Jesus, that You have redeemed me from the curse of the law, having been made a curse in my place. I sure didn't deserve that, but I am so thankful for it! Thank You for Your amazing sacrifice, and thank You, God, for allowing Your Son to take my place as well. I pray for others to truly understand the immense sacrifice that was made for us all.

How Beautiful Are the Feet of Those Who Preach the Gospel of Peace

"How beautiful are the feet of those who preach the gospel of peace, who bring glad tidings of good things!" (Romans 10:17).

What do you think this verse is referring to? I will start off by telling you what it is not referring to, and that is peace between men. I know that I have already ruffled some feathers, but I must speak the truth. In a perfect world, there would be world peace. But we don't live in a perfect world; we live in a fallen world, and the Bible says that in end times, there will be wars and rumors of wars (Matthew 24:6). We are in those end times, and peace on earth is not going to get any better. Even Jesus said He did not come to bring peace on earth, but a sword (Matthew 10:34). Until the return of Jesus, there will always be the battle of good versus evil, the kingdom of God versus the kingdom of this world. Christians will continue to be persecuted by non-Christians.

Please don't get depressed. That was not my intent; I was just proving a point. Now for the good news. What this verse is referring to when it talks about the gospel of peace is peace between God and man. That is the good news. Luke 2:13–14 says, "And suddenly there was with the angel a multitude of heavenly host praising God and saying: 'Glory to God in the highest, And on earth peace, goodwill toward men!'" Once again, this verse isn't referring to world peace but rather peace and goodwill from God toward men. This baby would grow up to be a man, become our sacrifice, and pay the price for all the sins of the entire world. He would appease the wrath of God and be the bridge of peace from God toward man. Praise the Lord!

Isaiah 53 and 54 are incredible prophetic chapters. Chapter 53 talks about the suffering of Jesus and all the things He would suffer on His body for us. In chapter 54, it talks about how the relationship between God and man would change after this. Isaiah 54:10 reads, "'For the mountains shall depart and the hills be removed, But My kindness shall not depart from you, nor shall my covenant of peace be removed,' says the Lord, who has mercy on you."

This is the glad tidings of good things from God to us. Because of the sacrifice of Jesus, we have peace with God. God is no longer angry because all the penalty for sin has been placed on the body of that innocent lamb, Jesus our Lord. Colossians 1:20 says, "And by Him to reconcile all things to Himself, by Him, whether things on earth or things in heaven, having made peace through the blood of His cross." What great news.

Do you want to have peace with God? God has done His part in this peace treaty by providing Jesus for us. Our part is to receive it by faith by making Jesus Lord of our lives. Romans 5:1 says, "Therefore, having been justified by faith, we have peace with God through our Lord Jesus Christ."

Here's an example to illustrate this truth: Let's say I bought you a house, no strings attached. It is all paid for. I have the keys to the house and am ready to hand them over to you, but you won't take them. That would be crazy, wouldn't it? Of course it would. That is the same thing with nonbelievers who won't accept the incredible free gift that Jesus sacrificed to give us all. The price has been paid; all you have to do is receive by faith.

If you have never received Jesus as your Lord and would like to, I encourage you to pray this prayer from your mouth and believe it with all your heart:

> Lord Jesus, I thank You for taking my place, for being a sacrifice for me. I want to live for You; I make You my Lord and Savior. I receive this free gift that You have provided for me through the innocent blood You shed for me. Thank You, Jesus, for forgiving my sins and coming into my heart. Amen.

If you prayed that prayer, welcome to the kingdom! You are now officially a child of God and a joint heir with Christ. Your spirit has been changed, and you now have the spirit of Jesus living inside you.

During this Christmas season, I encourage everyone to reflect on the wonder of our Savior. Take time to thank Him for His amazing sacrifice that made peace with God available to us all.

I love those verses in Isaiah. Such comfort in knowing that God will never be angry with us and will always be at peace with us, and it is all because of Jesus! People need to catch hold of this because too many people have a wrong view of God and are still under the old covenant mind-set. We should not be preaching condemnation anymore. There has been a change, and it is all because of Jesus!

God Has Not Given Us a Spirit of Fear

There is a lot of fear in the world today, even among believers. It seems everywhere you go or anything you hear has an element of fear attached to it. But God does not want us to live in fear. Fear is not from God. The Bible says that "God has not given us a spirit of fear, but of power and of love and of a sound mind" (2 Timothy 1:7).

I have heard from a few people that when I talk about Satan and things happening out of God's will, it causes fear to rise up on the inside of them. That was not my intent. Although I don't enjoy talking about Satan, I do so because I want people to be aware of him and his tactics. Too many people are ignorant in this area. I *do not*, however, want believers to be scared of him or make him the focus of their attention. I want believers to know that he has been defeated. When Jesus rose from the grave He bought back the power to believers that Adam lost in the garden. I want people to know the exceeding greatness of His power toward us. Jesus didn't hoard His power and keep it to Himself when He went to heaven. No, He passed it along to everyone who receives Him as their Savior.

The apostle Paul had revelation of this power. That is why in Ephesians 1:17–21 he prayed for the believers that "[God] may give to you the spirit of wisdom and revelation in the knowledge of Him, the eyes of your understanding being enlightened; that you may know what is the hope of His calling, what are the riches of the glory of His inheritance in the saints, and what is the exceeding greatness of His power toward us who believe, according to the working of His mighty power which He worked in Christ when He raised Him from the dead and seated Him at His right hand in heavenly places, far above all principality and power and might and dominion, and every name that is named, not only in this age but also in that which is to come."

Paul prayed that they would know about this incredible power that is in each born again believer, the same power that was used to raise Jesus from the dead and defeat the devil. Just think of what incredible power that had to be.

Paul knew about this power, and He used it regularly. He knew who He was in Christ and what power He had as a Christ follower. Paul did not live a mediocre, powerless Christian life, and he didn't want us to either.

James 4:7 tells us to "resist the devil, and he will flee from you." Note, it doesn't tell us to ask God to resist him for us; it tells us to resist. To resist means to actively fight against. God wouldn't have told us to do this if He didn't give us the power to do so.

I used to live with a lot of fear. I was scared of bad things happening all the time. And bad things did happen to me a lot. Instead of resisting the devil and standing on the Word to get him to flee from me, I, through my ignorance, unknowingly opened up the door so he could just come right in. I didn't know about this authority that I had been given as a believer. But now that I know this power, I am not scared anymore. And what freedom that is! I know that He (Jesus) who is in me is greater than he (Satan) who is in the world (1 John 4:4). I know that no weapon formed against me shall prosper (Isaiah 54:17). I know that as Jesus is, so am I in this world (1 John 4:17). I choose to meditate on these verses and declare them out loud, and when I do so that spirit of power rises up on the inside of me, and the fear fades.

I pray for my readers to get a hold of this. I encourage you to meditate on some of the scriptures I have mentioned and pray that prayer for yourself that Paul prayed for the people of Ephesus. The more we know God and understand this incredible power we have been given, the more we will live the power-filled life Jesus died for us to have. Doesn't that sound better than living a mediocre, fearful Christian life? It sure does to me!

Stay tuned for more on this subject next week.

I used to watch the news a lot, but I've quit because all they try to do is invoke fear into people. I want to do everything I can to keep those fearful ideas and attitudes from entering my mind and the minds of my family. As believers, we shouldn't live in fear, and I want to help others who are struggling in this area as I used to. I had no idea about how powerful the word of God was, and now that I know, it has certainly changed my perspective on things.

The Most Powerful Weapon We Have in Our Battle against Fear

In our battle against fear, we need the best weapon we can get. Just like soldiers need weapons when they go off to battle, we need weapons as well in our battle against fear. The best weapon we can possibly use is the word of God. This is the weapon Jesus used when He was tempted by Satan in the wilderness. Every time Satan tempted Him, Jesus countered the temptation with "it is written" and then quoted scripture. So whenever Satan tempts us to get into fear, shouldn't we follow the example of Jesus and use the word of God as well?

Hebrews 4:12 says, "For the word of God is living and powerful, and sharper than any two-edged sword." Sounds like a pretty powerful weapon, doesn't it? We, as believers, need to utilize this amazing weapon we have been given.

The word of God has so many promises in it, yet few believers grab hold of those promises and claim them as their own. I think most think that, yes, it says that, but how can we really believe it? Let me ask you, if the person you trusted the most in the entire world promised you something, would you believe it? Sad thing is, most people would believe their best friend or spouse over what God says. It is impossible for God to lie. I have heard someone once say that faith is taking God at His word. I love that simple yet powerful definition. How many of us are taking God at His word? Or are we trusting in what we can see instead? Faith is believing in what we can't see. We are to walk by faith, not by sight (2 Corinthians 5:7). But sadly many walk by sight, and then they have faith. That is what Thomas did when he refused to believe Jesus was alive until he saw with his own eyes. How did Jesus reply to him? In John 20:29, Jesus said, "Thomas, because you have seen Me, you have believed. Blessed are those who have not seen and yet have believed."

So how do we use this powerful weapon we have been given? When fear rises in me, I know I need to renew my mind and counter the fear with what the Word says. I tell myself, "Okay, this fear is not from God. God didn't give me a spirit of fear, but of love, power, and sound mind!" I then find scriptures declaring what God has promised to me as a believer and meditate on them.

For example, let's say you are in a financial bind. The enemy wants you to become fearful, yet God wants you to believe that He is going to take care of you. The Bible promises that "my God shall supply all your needs according to His riches in glory" (Philippians 4:19). Psalms 34:10 says, "The young lions lack and suffer hunger, but those who seek the Lord shall not lack any good thing." Trust in those words. Our job is not to figure out how it is going to happen; we are to trust the *Who* behind the how. That is faith.

Psalms 91 is packed full of promises that are available to every believer. Practically every day I pray verses 10 to 12 over my family. It reads, "No evil shall befall you, nor shall any plague come near your dwelling; for He shall give His angels charge over you, to keep you in all your ways, in their hands they shall bear you up, lest you dash your foot against a stone."

If people start talking about getting sick, I start speaking the Word. No plague shall come near my dwelling. No evil shall befall us. There is such peace in knowing the power we have been given as believers to the promises of God.

Now I would dare to bet that most people think I am crazy or fanatical when they read this. But I think it is crazy not to grab hold of these promises God has given us in the Bible. God does not want us to live in fear. He wants us to walk boldly in faith.

Is there an area of your life in which you are living in fear? I encourage you to fight that fear with the word of God. Find a few scriptures that are applicable to your situation, meditate on them, and declare them aloud by faith. I promise you this: the more you allow the word of God to become real to you, the less fear you will have. How do I know? I am living proof of it. And I want you to be as well.

Stacie wrote, "Another amazing article, Amber. That one definitely spoke to my heart. Thank you for these."

Oh how I long for the children of God to catch hold of the Word of God and to hold onto the promises in it! Don't live in fear. Live in the Word! There is so much power in the Word!

Death and Life Are in the Power of the Tongue

> Death and life are in the power of the tongue, and those who love it will eat its fruit.
>
> —Proverbs 18:21

What kinds of words do you speak over yourself? Did you know that words are powerful? Your tongue can prohibit the blessings of God from flowing in your life. Some people get frustrated when bad things happen to them, yet a lot of those bad things are spoken into existence through their negative talk. Their words become a self-fulfilling prophecy. Stop cursing yourself with your own words. As the above verse mentions, life and death are in the power of the tongue. Whatever you speak over yourself, you will eat the fruit of it. Learn to speak blessings over your life.

I used to be clueless as to the importance of our words. I spoke bad things over myself and my life all the time. I distinctly remember one time, about ten years ago, when life was going relatively smooth at the moment. I opened my big mouth and proclaimed, "Things are going good right now. Well, I'm sure something bad will happen soon." And something bad did happen then. I can't remember what it was, but I remember thinking, "See, I was right. I knew something bad would happen because things were going too good." It didn't dawn on me that the bad thing most likely happened because I put faith in that happening and spoke it into existence.

Do you know that you can have faith in bad things happening just like you can have faith in good things happening? When we believe and speak bad things over our life we are putting faith in that happening and opening up a door for the devil to just march right into our lives. Now don't get into fear; I am making this point so you can be aware and put a watch over your mouth.

My dear father was just as clueless as I was as to the importance of our words. The last couple years of his life, he starting saying that he would probably get cancer and die before he could enjoy his retirement. I don't know why he said those things. Cancer did not run in his family. But guess what happened? He got cancer and died at the age of sixty-four before he was able to retire. Some people call that a coincidence. I believe it is because life and death are in the power of the tongue.

Before we can speak right, however, we first need to believe right. Do you believe God is for you or against you? Many people haven't had the revelation that God is truly for them, so they believe and speak contrary to that. They say negative things over themselves instead of positive because they don't know how much God loves them and wants to bless them. They actually hinder the blessings of God through their wrong beliefs and words.

God is for you and wants good for all of us. Do not be deceived (as so many are); He only gives us good gifts (James 1:16–17). The Third Epistle of John 1:2 reads, "Beloved, I pray that you may prosper in all things and be in health, just as your soul prospers." John 10:10 says that Jesus came that you may have life, and have it more abundantly. Jeremiah 29:11 states that God's plans are to prosper you, not to harm you, to give you a hope and a future.

I'm here to tell you that God does not want you to be sick, depressed, and poor. He wants you to live the abundant life that His Son died to give you. You need to get that foundation rooted deep in your heart. It wasn't until I started believing God was really for me that I could speak it from my lips. "Out of the abundance of the heart the mouth speaks" (Matthew 12:34). Words reveal what we really believe in our hearts.

My life has been full of blessings from God the past seven years, and I believe it is because I finally allowed myself to receive from God and didn't hinder those blessings through wrong beliefs and destructive words. I now speak blessings over my life because I know that is what God wants for me. And He wants it for you as well. I pray for each of you reading this that you will know how much God wants to bless you. (See Deuteronomy 28:1–13 for a list of ways God wants to bless you.) I also pray you will learn that life and death are in the power of the tongue. Knowing this can truly change the course of your life!

A lady named Kathleen wrote, Good morning, Amber:

I wanted to e-mail you this morning to say that I believe God used your article from last week to prepare my heart for a couple other things He wanted to show me. I am very grateful that you wrote that article ("Power of the Tongue").

Another reader named Marsha wrote, "Love your message in the Bargain Hunter *this week! I'm a believer!"*

Martha wrote, "This is so amazing. These were my thoughts today. Gen 1: God created us in His image, God spoke and it was. Therefore if God's words have power, so do ours. God wants us to speak positive into our own lives and others. Our words are powerful…and then I come across your article. That's called God-timing. Couldn't agree more with your article.

Praise God! Father, I pray for others to understand the power of our tongues as well. I pray for an awareness to arise in the hearts and minds of believers to what they are actually saying, and may they use their words wisely to speak life into their own lives as well as the lives of others.

One Conversation I Wish I Could Redo

A few years ago, a relative of mine accepted Jesus as his Savior. It was very exciting for me to hear of that happening, and I got a chance to talk with him after his conversion. He had some concerns, however, because he had been living a sinful lifestyle and didn't know how he could change his ways completely. He was told by some since he was now a Christian, he couldn't do the things he had been doing before. There was a list of dos and don'ts that he was to adhere to. I wasn't sure what to tell him at the time because yes, those things that he had been doing were sins. Those choices were definitely not God's best for him. But when we are given a list of things we have to do when we become a Christian, it puts us in bondage. It leads to condemnation when we mess up. It puts us back under the law mentality that we have to do everything right to please God and places the burden back on our shoulders.

If I had it to do over, I would tell him something like this: I am all for right living. Yes, the lifestyle that you have been living isn't one that brings glory to God, and it definitely isn't the best for you. But I don't want you to focus on that. I don't want you to look at everything you need to do. Instead, I want you to look at Jesus and everything He has done for you. Proverbs 37:3 says to "dwell in the land, and feed on His faithfulness." I want you to feed on the faithfulness of Jesus. Notice, it doesn't say feed on your faithfulness to Him. But when you feed on His faithfulness to you, your faithfulness to Him will come as a byproduct of receiving His faithfulness to you just like your love for Him will come when you know how much He loves you

(1 John 4:19). Draw from the fact that this innocent Jesus not only took our sins, but in return gave us His righteousness (2 Corinthians 5:21). It doesn't say He gave us His righteousness (right standing with God) when we do everything right. None of us will ever do everything right. Even when we are in the midst of messing up He is still imputing His righteousness toward us. Did we do anything to deserve that? No, we didn't. That is the grace of God. It is His unearned, undeserved, unmerited favor toward us. When you meditate on that fact, it will empower you to live a victorious life for Jesus. Instead of pushing away God's love because you don't feel good enough or that you don't deserve it, it will allow you to receive His incredible love for you. Many people push Jesus away after they have sinned because they don't feel worthy to receive His love. The fact is, none of us, in and of ourselves, are deserving of God's love. But that didn't stop Jesus from hanging on that cross for all of us, and He did it "while we were still sinners" (Romans 5:8). Allow Jesus to love you right where you are at. Feed on His amazing love for you by getting in the Word and soaking it all up. I can tell you from experience, when you allow God to love you and don't push Him away because you don't think you are good enough, your natural response will be to love Jesus in return.

You know those bad habits that you think you won't be able to break? When you keep your eyes on Jesus and get into His word, He will change your desires. Psalms 37:4 says, "Delight yourself in the Lord, and He will give you the desires of your heart." That means that He will literally put His desires into your heart. Second Corinthians 3:18 states, "But we all, with unveiled face, beholding as in a mirror the glory of the Lord, are being transformed into the same image from glory to glory, just as by the spirit of the Lord."

When you behold Jesus and His grace and love toward you, He will transform you. So don't fight in your own strength to break those bad habits or look at all you have to do now that you are a Christian. The main thing I want you to do is just allow Jesus to love you and always keep your focus on Him!

This had been on my heart for a while, especially after one of my high school friends got saved. I made sure to tell her that it is all about what Jesus has done for us and not about what we have to do for Him. When we realize what He has done for us, that will lead us to live right.

I e-mailed my cousin that I wrote this about and gave him the link to this article. I think he had kind of drifted in his relationship with God and then came back, and I believe it was probably because there was so much pressure on him to live right. He responded with, "Wow. That really touched me on a deep level. That is really awesome."

I told him I just wish I would have known this earlier so I could have told him this right after he got saved. We as Christians need to get our beliefs right first, which will cause us to live right. It isn't the other way around. Boy, what a change from what I used to believe! I pray others will understand this as well.

There Is No Condemnation to Those Who Are in Christ Jesus

Do you ever feel condemned, like you are not ever good enough? I used to live in an almost perpetual state of condemnation (with a little self-righteousness thrown in here and there). I was condemned if I did and condemned if I didn't. It seemed like I was just never good enough. I would read my Bible and get condemned because I didn't seem to measure up to God's standard. I would play sports and be condemned because I messed up one too many times and could have made a few more shots. When I was around people, I would be condemned because I should have said something different or I shouldn't have spoken at all. I was always looking at myself and how I didn't measure up. My focus was always on me. *Looking at ourselves instead of Jesus will always result in either condemnation or self-righteousness.*

Without being aware of it (and I wouldn't have known what this meant even if you had told me), I had a law-based mentality. Under the Old Testament law (meaning the Ten Commandments and the ordinances following it), you were always condemned. When you sinned, you had to offer up a sacrifice for your sin. That just temporarily covered your sin; it didn't take it away. Sin was always on your mind. The law was to make sin come alive in you and for you to die (Romans 7:9). It was to make you see your need for a Savior (Galatians 3:24).

Did you know the Ten Commandments were called the ministry of condemnation? Now I know that most people don't believe me, but let me show you from God's word.

Second Corinthians 3:9 reads, "For if the ministry of condemnation had glory, the ministry of righteousness exceeds much more in glory."

If you read the previous verses, the whole thing is talking about the Ten Commandments, because in verse 3 it says, "Clearly you are an epistle of Christ, ministered by us, written not with ink but by the Spirit of the living God, not on tablets of stone but on tablets of flesh, that is, of the heart." What was written on tablets of stone? The Ten Commandments! Verse 7 even calls it the ministry of death, written and engraved on stones. Verse 6 says that the letter kills, but the spirit gives life.

Am I throwing a loophole in anyone's theology yet? What is the point am I trying to make? Glad you asked. My point is, under the law people's focus was always on themselves and what they had to do. They had to earn God's approval through their works. They were blessed if they did everything right. If not, they were cursed. We are not to have this mentality anymore, although I think it is prevalent in many Christian circles, like it was for me. We aren't to look to ourselves but look to Jesus. Romans 8:1 says, "There is therefore now no condemnation to those who are in Christ Jesus, who do not walk according to the flesh but according to the Spirit."

If you have received Jesus as your Savior, you should not feel condemned. God isn't the one putting those condemning thoughts in your head, saying that you aren't good enough. They are either from yourself because you are ignorant of this truth or from the enemy, trying to get you back under condemnation.

I can't put into words what knowing this truth has done for me. When I received revelation of it from the Holy

Spirit, it was like these heavy chains that had weighed me down for so many years just fell from my body. That is one of the reasons I am so on fire for Jesus because I am so thankful for what He has done for me. When I sin, I don't have to grovel in the dirt anymore, hang my head, and beat myself up. I can still come boldly to the throne of grace (Hebrews 4:6).

I have learned so much about this and want to see others set free as well. I will be expanding more on this topic, so stay tuned!

I was excited to write this article because it was written from my experience, and I believed it would hit home with others. I got more positive e-mails about this article than any other article. Many people struggle with condemnation because religion has preached the old covenant of law instead of the new covenant of grace. This confirmed to me that grace, not condemnation, is what people are needing and longing to hear. It was also the article that opened up doors to new friendships with other believers who also believed in this good news, and for that, I am ever so grateful.

A lady named Kathy wrote, "Thanks so much for your recent article on condemnation. You described me exactly. Just recently, my husband and I have been discussing this very thing. I told him I know it's true in my head but have such a hard time believing it in my heart and not wallowing in guilt. I have accepted condemnation as conviction. I have felt in the past few days like the chains are breaking from me as well, and your article just broke a few more links!

Praise the Lord! May others be set free as well when they read this!

The Old Covenant of Law versus the New Covenant of Grace

"There is therefore now no condemnation to those who are in Christ Jesus, who do not walk according to the flesh, but according to the Spirit" (Romans 8:1).

As this verse mentions, if we are born-again believers through faith in Jesus, God is no longer condemning us. If feelings and thoughts of condemnation rise up against us, we need to fight them, not by justifying ourselves through what we have done, but rather by what Jesus has done for us. In order to be able to do this, we need to get a firm grasp of the new covenant of grace compared to the old covenant of the law.

John 1:17 says, "For the law was given through Moses, but grace and truth came through Jesus Christ." See how this verse is contrasting what came through Moses and what came through Jesus? There is a huge difference between the old covenant of law, which was given to Moses by God, and the new covenant of grace, which came through Jesus.

I would guess that a lot of people haven't heard much about this or understand what it all means. I used to be clueless on the subject. I would read through books of the Bible like Romans and Galatians and not have any idea what all this law stuff meant. Anyone with me on that? But now that I've learned about the difference between the old covenant (law) and the new covenant (grace), I love reading about it. Romans and Galatians have become my two favorite books in the Bible. These books reveal the wonderful gift of undeserved favor that we have been given through the sacrifice of Jesus, and it is all about what He has done for us, not what we do for Him. I will try to do my best to explain these covenants and pray for the Holy Spirit to give revelation to everyone who reads this.

First, we need to understand why God gave the law and what purpose it served. The law wasn't God's first choice, or He would have slapped it on Adam and Eve right away. He showed mercy before the law (sin is not imputed where there is no law), but it got to a point where the Israelites were out of control. They were full of self-righteousness and ungrateful for all that God had done for them. They basically wanted God to give them a few rules and then leave them alone. They didn't see their need for God or a Savior; they thought they could handle things on their own. That's when the law came.

So despite what most people probably think, the Ten Commandments weren't a blessing. It wasn't "God's ten ways that we can be made right with him." It was actually the opposite; it was to make us see that we could *never* be right with God through our own works. Colossians 2:14 calls them the "handwriting of requirements that was against us." They are also referred to as the letter that kills, the ministry of death, and the ministry of condemnation (2 Corinthians 3:6, 7:9).

Galatians 3:19, 22–25 says, "What purpose then does the law serve? It was added because of transgressions, till the Seed should come to whom the promise was made.... But the Scripture has confined all under sin, that the promise by faith in Jesus Christ might be given to those who believe. But before faith came, we were kept under guard by the law; kept for the faith which would afterward be revealed. Therefore the law was our tutor to bring us to

Christ, that we might be justified by faith. But after faith has come, we are no longer under the law."

The law was to condemn us and break us of this self-righteous attitude of thinking we could justify ourselves. It pointed us to the only one that could justify us, and that was Jesus. After we have faith in Jesus, we are no longer to base our relationship with God on what we have to do, but we are to look to the One who has done it all for us. I hope this is starting to make sense, although it has probably raised a lot of questions as well. I have referenced a lot of scriptures, and I hope you will look them up for yourselves and pray for the Holy Spirit to give you revelation.

I am just scratching the surface and have a lot more to write about this topic. Stay tuned; you won't want to miss it!

I had wanted to write about this for a long time and knew it would take me quite a few articles to get through it. I am sure many of you reading this have never heard these truths before, like I hadn't until recently. There is so much confusion in the body of Christ and wrong doctrine promoting the law. The law was good and holy, but we could never keep it. Those who think they can are only deceiving themselves. Oh, how I love to hear about our new covenant of grace through Jesus. He saved us and sacrificed for us when we didn't deserve it, and knowing that makes me fall more in love with Him every day. The law didn't change hearts. People still sinned under the law because it made the desire for sin come alive in them. But when we understand grace and the sacrifice for Jesus, it frees us from that bondage of sin. We need to hear more about the new covenant of grace we are under because it will radically change lives!

What Remains Is Much More Glorious

I have been talking about the old covenant (law), as compared to the new covenant of grace, and in the past two articles I have primarily focused on the old covenant. The law was a conditional covenant, which means it was based on performance. You were only blessed if you followed the law. If you did good, you were rewarded. If you messed up, you were punished. You had to try to earn your righteousness through your behavior.

If we are born again, we are not to be living with this kind of mentality anymore. By putting faith in Jesus, we are now righteous; it isn't based on our works but rather on the work He did for us. Romans 10:4 states, "For Christ is the end of the law for righteousness to everyone who believes."

In this article, I want to make it very clear from scripture that the old covenant of law has passed away for believers, and we are now under the new covenant of grace (Romans 6:15). I think it is vitally important because I see people all around who don't understand this and are still trying to appease God through their works.

Hebrews 8:6–9, 13 states, "But now He has obtained a more excellent ministry, inasmuch as He is also Mediator of a better covenant, which was established on better promises. For if that first covenant had been faultless, then no place would have been sought for a second. Because finding fault with them, He says: 'Behold, the days are coming, says the Lord, when I will make a new covenant with the house of Israel and with the house of Judah—not according to the covenant that I made with their fathers… because they did not continue in My covenant, and I disregarded them,' says the Lord… For I will be merciful to their unrighteousness, and their sins and their lawless deeds I will remember no more. In that He says, 'A new covenant,' He has made the first obsolete. Now what is becoming obsolete and growing old is ready to vanish away."

After we put faith in Jesus, we are freed from the law because we are trusting in His righteousness, not our own. Romans 7:6 says, "But now we have been delivered from the law, having died to what we were held by, so that we should serve in the newness of the Spirit and not in the oldness of the letter."

Since none of us could keep the law perfectly, Christ has fulfilled the righteous requirement of the law for us (Romans 8:4). Because of Him, we are no longer under that conditional covenant of law but now under an unconditional covenant of grace through the blood of Jesus, the unearned, undeserved, unmerited favor of God through faith in Jesus.

Second Corinthians 3:6, 9, 11 says, "Who also made us sufficient as ministers of the new covenant, not of the letter but of the Spirit, for the letter kills, but the Spirit gives life. For if the ministry of condemnation had glory, the ministry of righteousness exceeds much more in glory. For if what is passing away was glorious, what remains is much more glorious."

The ministry of righteousness is talking about the new covenant, in which we are righteous with God through faith in Jesus. What a change. Now, it is no longer about what we have to do but about what He has done for us. The law demanded; grace freely gives. This is the gospel, the good news, and it is all because of Jesus. This is what we need to be sharing with people. We need to let them know that if they have made Jesus their Savior, they are right with God because of Him through faith, and God is not mad at them or condemning them. Romans 10:15 says, "How beautiful are the feet of those who preach the gospel of peace, who bring glad tidings of good things!" Note, it doesn't say the gospel of condemnation, which is so much of what we hear today. Instead of hearing about what we have to do, we need to hear about what Jesus has already done.

When we begin to fathom this incredible gift of grace, that came through Jesus when we did nothing to earn it or deserve it, that right believing will cause us to live right. And you know that law that we used to try to keep? Well, when our hearts are changed through believing in what Jesus has done for us, we will follow it better unintentionally by keeping our eyes on Him than we ever did on purpose before.

I am so thankful that Christ has redeemed us from the law and ushered in the new covenant of grace. What a change has occurred in me through learning these truths. When people understand what Jesus did for us, it radically changes their lives. It frees them to live fully for God without fear of rejection or wrath. Being free from the law doesn't mean we should go out and live in sin. No, when we understand we are not under the law but under grace, hearts change, and our motivation for right living goes from being motivated by fear to being motivated by love. Love is a much better motivator than fear. Rules don't change hearts but love does!

The Glory of the New Covenant

I'm excited to write this article because I get to talk about the good stuff. What is the good stuff? Everything that Jesus provided for us on the cross. This is important information that everyone needs to hear because very few people realize all the benefits that Jesus died on the cross to give us. Psalms 103:2 tells us not to forget all His benefits. I will try to explain some of these benefits.

As I have mentioned before, since no one could fulfill the righteous requirement of the law, God sent Jesus to fulfill it for us (Romans 8:3). That is how the old covenant could pass away because it was fulfilled by Jesus. Jesus redeemed us from the curse of the law, having been made a curse for us (Galatians 3:13). We will never be cursed for not fulfilling the law, because Jesus was already cursed for us.

When we have faith in Jesus, God is no longer condemning us, even when we sin. How can that be? Because God already condemned sin in the flesh of Jesus (Romans 8:4). He was condemned, so we wouldn't have to be. If God already condemned His Son, whom He loved so much, He isn't going to punish and condemn us for the same thing. The sacrifice of Jesus was enough. He forgives all our iniquities (Psalm 103:3).

Jesus not only became sin for us but in return gave us His righteousness (2 Corinthians 5:21). Isn't that amazing? Instead of having to try to earn our righteousness like we did under the old covenant, it is freely given to us by faith in Jesus under the new covenant. Hallelujah!

Psalm 103:3 also goes on to say that He heals all our disease. This is a benefit that few people realize, but what a wonderful benefit it is. Jesus bore every sickness and disease on His body so we wouldn't have to. The First Epistle of Peter 2:24 says that "by whose stripes you were healed." This is not just talking about spiritual healing, but physical healing and healing in every area of your life where you need it. God didn't want to see any of us suffer, just like we don't want to see any of our children suffer, so He sent Jesus in our place to suffer for us. Jesus bore our griefs, sorrows, transgressions, iniquities, infirmities, and sicknesses on His body so we wouldn't have to (Isaiah 53:4-5, Matthew 8:17). Healing is part of the atonement of Christ. I'm telling you, folks, Jesus is the real deal. He's the complete package.

I know people are resisting that last paragraph. You are probably thinking, "How can that be? So many people are sick today?" Hosea 4:6 says, "My people are destroyed for lack of knowledge." How many people know and believe in this benefit? Many people think that God puts sickness on them to teach them a lesson. Others believe that He might want to heal someone or He might not. Remember, things happen out of God's will, and it is His will for everyone to be healed. 3 John 2, it says, "Beloved, I pray that you may prosper in all things and be in health, just as your soul prospers." God wants us to prosper in every area of our life. Period. He has already provided healing and everything else we will need through the sacrifice of His Son. Our part is to receive these benefits by faith. *Our faith doesn't move God; our faith reaches out and receives what Jesus has already freely provided for us on the cross.*

People have a hard time believing these truths because they don't know the depth of God's love for us. We look at ourselves and don't think God would ever want to do those things for us. We think of God's love like it is conditional human love, that He only loves us and gives us things if we are worthy to receive them. But God's love is just the opposite. He has done everything for us and keeps doing for us when we aren't worthy. It is a free gift. This is the unearned, undeserved, unmerited favor of God toward us through His Son Jesus. Grace cannot be earned, only freely received.

If everyone could grasp the extent of our Daddy's amazing love, this love that passes mere human understanding, we would have no trouble believing that He wants nothing but the best for us. We need to get our eyes off ourselves and our unworthiness and look to Jesus, who died to make us worthy. God sacrificed His absolute best for us: His beloved Son. I pray for you to believe in that and to receive everything that Jesus died to give you. This is the glory of the new covenant!

I was nervous to write on this because I touched a lot on healing. Many people are either misinformed about this or very resistant to it. But I told the Lord I will write whatever He calls me to write no matter what. I was disappointed that I got virtually no feedback. Once again, it is not about me receiving praise but rather people understanding what Jesus did for us all! He died for our healing just as much as He died for our sins. I want people to understand this and catch hold of it. Jesus died so we wouldn't have to live sick like the rest of the world. I pray for Christians to get revelation of this and to get sick and tired of being sick and tired!

My one friend Sheila did write me and say that she read this article over several times, trying to get a deeper understanding and revelation of it.

Father, even if just one person learns this, then it is worth it, but I pray for the spirit of wisdom and revelation in the knowledge of You to be upon all believers who read it.

Are You a Spiritual Double-Dipper?

I used to double-dip a lot. Yes, I know this is an awful habit, but honestly, I didn't know any better. No one had ever told me the truth that I shouldn't do it. Since I have learned how wrong it is, I want to teach you all as well because I know that the vast majority of Christians reading this are double-dippers as well. Spiritual double-dippers, that is.

What is this crazy woman talking about?

Glad you asked.

I am talking about dipping into Jesus (grace) and then dipping back into our works (law). Looking back, I was the chief of the double-dippers. I knew that I needed Jesus to get to heaven (dipping into grace), but then after that, I thought my right standing with God was dependent upon me (dipping back into the law). My relationship with God had to do with a little bit of what Jesus had done but *a lot* of what I had to do. Little dip into Jesus, *big* dip into my works.

The people of Galatia were big-time spiritual double-dippers as well. They received Jesus, then fell for lies that they needed to go back under the law to be righteous. Hmm, sound familiar? Galatians 3:3 says, "Are you so foolish? Having begun in the Spirit, are you now being made perfect by the flesh?"

Paul, through inspiration of the Holy Spirit, is addressing this issue of spiritual double-dipping. Basically, Paul is telling them, "Why are you thinking you need to add to what Jesus has already done? You can't add to it, and there is no way you can earn your righteousness. Your righteousness is not dependent upon you but dependent upon Jesus. Stop double-dipping and dip only into Jesus."

Galatians 2:16 reads, "Knowing that a man is not justified by works of the law but by faith in Jesus Christ, even we have believed in Christ Jesus, that we might be justified by faith in Christ and not by the works of the law; for by the works of the law no flesh shall be justified." Faith in Jesus is what justifies us.

Abraham lived before the law was even given. Do you know what made him righteous in God's eyes? Was it all his mighty works? No. Galatians 3:6 says, "Just as Abraham 'believed God, and it was accounted to him for righteousness.'" His belief is what made him righteous, just like our belief (faith) in Jesus is what makes us righteous.

Second Corinthians 5:21 has become one of my favorite verses. It reads, "For He made Him who knew no sin to be sin for us, that we might become the righteousness of God in Him." When I truly got revelation of this verse, it blew me away. I remember thinking, *You mean Jesus not only took* all *my sins, but also* gave *me His righteousness? And now I am righteous in God's eyes because I have faith in Jesus and not because of my works? How can this be? Why haven't I heard this before?* The more I read my Bible, the more I saw scripture after scripture after scripture confirming this truth. The stress and burden I felt from having to earn my righteousness through my actions faded away, and an overwhelming sense of love, peace, joy, and gratitude flooded my soul.

Now I can just rest in Jesus. I don't have to look at myself and all that I have to do. I just rest in the work that He has done for me. It has taken a lot of renewing of my mind to this truth and filtering out of the old garbage. I tell myself that I am the righteousness of God in Christ Jesus, fully knowing that truth isn't because of anything I have done but because of everything He has done for me. Since I know this truth, I have such a passion to serve my awesome Savior with every ounce of my entire being and tell others about this good news as well.

To all you spiritual double-dippers out there, I want to end this with a final word of scripture from Galatians 5:1: "Stand fast therefore in the liberty by which Christ has made us free, and do not be entangled again with a yoke of bondage."

Don't allow yourself to get back under the bondage of the law by focusing on yourself and your works. I encourage you to live free in this freedom Jesus died for you to have by keeping your eyes on Him and His righteousness. Stop the double-dipping and dip only into Jesus!

My friend Shannon shared my article on Facebook and wrote, "Please take a few minutes to read her article. It will change your life!"

A pastor at a local church wrote to me: "I just wanted to drop you a line and say I enjoyed your article. It was great to see the heart of the gospel expounded in our local paper. Many thanks!"

Thank You, Lord, for Your encouragement! I got the idea for this article many months ago but didn't feel called to write it until this point. I think the Christian realm is full of spiritual double-dippers, and I pray that people will realize it is not about us and what we do but all about Jesus and what He did for us! Don't mix your good works with Jesus. It is all about Jesus!

The True Meaning of the Sabbath Revealed

I just finished writing about the old covenant of law as compared to the new covenant of grace that we are now under if we have put faith in Jesus. So does that mean that the law is wrong and we can just go out and steal, murder, and commit adultery whenever we want? Of course not! The law is good and holy, but we are not to use the law to bring us to righteousness. We are to look to Jesus, who is our righteousness, and by keeping our eyes on Him and believing in His love for us, our hearts will be changed, and we will end up following the law better without even trying.

So with that being said, I want to talk about the true meaning of the Sabbath. I know this is going to get some people fired up, but God has put it on my heart to share about this, and I have learned to do what He tells me to do. I believe it will set some people free.

Under the old covenant, the Sabbath represented a day of the week that people were to refrain from all their work so they could focus on God and trust in His provision. The Sabbath was from sundown Friday to sundown Saturday. Many people who try to keep the Sabbath today aren't even doing so because the Sabbath was not Sunday.

This Sabbath that was represented under the old covenant was symbolic, a shadow of what was to come, meaning Jesus. Colossians 2:16–17 states, "So let no one judge you in food or in drink, or regarding a festival or a new moon or Sabbaths, which are a shadow of things to come, but the substance is of Christ."

Hebrews 4:4–5, 9–10 says, "For He has spoken in a certain place of the seventh day in this way: 'And God rested on the seventh day from all His works,' and again in this place: 'They shall not enter My rest [talking about the people of Israel].' Therefore remains a rest for the people of God. For he who has entered His rest has himself also ceased from his works as God did from His."

For the sake of space, I didn't write all the verses in between. This may sound confusing, but let me explain. Under the new covenant, the Sabbath is representing a relationship, not a day. Under the old covenant, the Sabbath was the day they ceased from their works, but now it is about a lifestyle of ceasing from our works (not talking physical work, so don't claim this as an opportunity for laziness). Now we are constantly to be resting in what Jesus has done for us and not trusting in our own works—resting in the fact that through faith in Him we are righteous with God and we don't have to try to earn it through our actions, trusting in Him to take care of us and provide for us and not us trying to do it in our own strength. It is about a relationship of continual rest in our Savior.

I used to be very hypocritical when it came to the Sabbath (or what I thought was the Sabbath). I would do work inside but not outside because I didn't want people to see me. I remember one time an old neighbor of mine who happened to be a preacher was mowing on a Sunday. I was appalled. "He is mowing on a Sunday, and he is a preacher?" I thought to myself. Well, I think that preacher man knew a lot more about the new covenant meaning of the Sabbath than I did!

Physical rest is good for our bodies, and I think taking a day off to relax is beneficial for us. But sometimes some "work" can be relaxing. I know of a guy who loves to mow. He wishes he could mow on Sundays and has questioned why, if it relaxes him, God wouldn't allow him to mow. As far as I know, he still doesn't mow on Sundays. I doubt the new covenant definition of the Sabbath has ever been explained to him. I sure hope he is reading this because I want him to know that God has given him the green light to mow away. Make sure to have plenty of copies of this article to hand out when people give judgmental looks so they can understand the true meaning of the Sabbath as well.

Remember, it's not about a day, but about a lifestyle. Ceasing from our works and trusting in the one who did the work for us—Jesus.

This was one topic God laid on my heart that I was hesitant to write because I knew I would receive criticism on it. And I did. So many people do what they do because they have always done it and don't know why they even do it. I don't know if the people who criticized me even tried to understand what I wrote. The Sabbath was symbolic of a relationship with Jesus, and now that Jesus has come, our Sabbath is in resting in His finished work, not just one day of the week. I think having an everyday attitude of the Sabbath rest in Jesus is better than just one day of the week!

One guy was not very nice at all and accused me of telling people they can go and sin because we are under grace. But praise God that I did get some positive feedback from people who truly understand that it isn't about us and what we do but about what Jesus has done for us.

One guy named Loren wrote me and said, "I read your article in the Bargain Hunter, *'The Sabbath Revealed.' Great article and the truth!"*

Jason commented, "Love it!"

It helped me to get encouragement after being criticized so badly.

Lord, I will keep preaching the truth though, no matter what persecution I may face!

I Love How You Love Me

In high school, I developed a love for oldies music, the good old songs from the fifties and sixties. Ask any of my friends from high school or college, and they will no doubt groan in remembrance of it. No one liked when I rode shotgun because they knew I would have control of the radio, which inevitably meant oldies music.

Anyhow, there was a 1961 hit by the Paris sisters entitled, "I Love How You Love Me." I often sing those words to my Lord in an act of praise and worship. "Father, I love how You love me." It is overwhelming to have the God of this universe love me unconditionally. He loves me through it all. When I succeed, when I fail, at all times, under all conditions, my Father loves me. I know I don't deserve it, yet He loves me anyway. And I *love* that. I love how He loves me.

Recently I was singing that to God, and I heard God speak back to me in my spirit so clearly and say, "Amber, I love that you let me love you." That really hit me. A few years back, I wouldn't have heard God say that to me because I would never have been singing that song to Him in the first place. I didn't have a revelation of how much God loves me. I thought I wasn't good enough and could never meet His standards. I pushed away God's love because I just didn't think I was worthy enough to deserve it.

I don't think I or anyone else will ever know how much God loves us, yet I have a much deeper grasp of it than I did before. He loves me so much that He gave up His only Son for me. I can't imagine giving up one of my sons, whom

I love so much, to be sacrificed for someone else. It makes me want to cry just thinking about it.

I can sing that now because I know the new covenant of grace, that God isn't basing His love for me on how good I am and whether I have done everything right. He is basing His love for me on the fact that He sees Jesus in me. This isn't because I am anything great, but rather that I have put faith in the one who is great; that is Jesus. The song I sing to the Lord is not one of pride or arrogance but rather a song of humility. If I thought I deserved God's love, I wouldn't be singing that to Him. Why would I be thankful for something that I thought I already had coming to me, something I deserved or had earned? I know this love is the undeserved, unearned, unmerited favor of God, and it is all because of Jesus. As Jesus is, so are we in this world (1 John 4:17). Is Jesus loved unconditionally by his Father? Yes. Then so am I. Isn't that good news? That's the gospel!

When God spoke those words to me, it also made me think of all the people who don't allow God to love them, just like I previously didn't. They look at themselves and all their shortcomings rather than looking at what Jesus did for them. Jesus died to make us accepted in the Beloved (Ephesians 1:6). God doesn't want us to take the sacrifice His Son made for granted. He wants us to receive what Jesus died to give us, and that is unconditional love from our Father through the blood of His Son.

I love to hug and kiss and cuddle with my little boys. But sometimes, they aren't in the mood for it and don't let me. And that hurts. I want to tell them not to push me away, just let me show my love for them. There is nothing that blesses me more than my children allowing me to show them love, and if one of those little guys would ever utter the words, "Mommy, I love how you love me," I think that would be the ultimate compliment I could ever receive as a mother.

I believe God, as our Heavenly Father, feels the same. Won't you receive His love for you today? Remember, He did not spare His own Son but gave Him up for you! There is no better way you can bless God than to allow yourself to be loved by Him. I pray that you will get to a place where you can sing those words to God as well, with a heart full of praise and thankfulness, "Father, I love how You love me!"

I remember exactly where it was when God spoke those words to me. I was driving to our lawyer's office, taking him the purchase and sale agreement the buyer signed for our old house. When God spoke that to me, I immediately thought, "That would make a great story." God is so good and gives me ideas when I am least expecting it, and for that, I am so thankful. When I first started writing, I submitted articles every other week because I just didn't think I could do it every week, with taking care of the boys and all. But I felt God tell me that I could do it and not to limit Him, so I have been doing it every week now. At first, I started stressing if I wasn't practically finished with my article a week in advance. As I have learned to rest in Him and trust Him more, there will be times when I have just a day or so before my cutoff, and I still don't know exactly what I am writing about. I've decided that stress puts the burden back on me, and God doesn't want that. He wants me to cast all my cares upon Him and then rely on Him to give me the answers I need.

Do for Someone What You Would Want Someone to Do for You

The other day, one of my friends shared about how someone had anonymously left a bag of groceries on her doorstep, for which she was ever so grateful. It was a huge blessing to her, and I was excited for her. One of her friends commented, "Boy, I wish someone would do that for me."

How selfish, I thought to myself. *Why don't you try doing that for someone else? Why don't you sow a seed of your own and maybe by planting a seed you will reap back what you have sown?*

A few days later, I read a blog a different friend wrote. She mentioned how one of her friends planned this all-day surprise for my friend's birthday. Her friend went out of her way to make my friend feel special and loved, paying attention to little details that she knew my friend would enjoy.

I was happy for her, but I have to admit that a selfish, jealous, self-pitying side of me also came out, one of which I am not proud. After reading that, I said to myself, *I wish someone would do something nice like that for me on my birthday.*

Yes, I know, it was like the pot calling the kettle black. Hypocrite with a capital H. I am not proud of my response, but I am being totally honest.

After I said that, I really felt God impress upon my heart, "Whatever you would like someone to do for you,

you do it for someone else." That hit so deep into my being. It wasn't God condemning me but rather encouraging me to be a blessing for someone. God spoke the golden rule right into my life. Luke 6:31 says, "And just as you want men to do to you, you also do to them likewise."

I think a lot of the time we use that verse in a negative sense—like if you don't want someone to say something mean to you, don't say something mean to them. But how about we use it from a positive point of view? Think of something nice that you would want someone to do for you, and you do it for someone else.

After I got over my selfish spell and received God's word, it made me excited. I knew of someone who had a birthday coming up the next day, and I wanted to be able to be a blessing to that person. It made me feel good to be able to do something nice for her. Focusing on someone else pulled me out of that self-pitying attitude. By blessing her, it blessed me. I think it blessed God as well because He loves to see His children blessed. Matthew 25:40 says, "And the King will answer and say to them, 'Assuredly, I say to you, inasmuch as you did it to one of the least of these My brethren, you did it to Me.'"

I encourage you to sow seeds of love into someone else's life. Think of what would bless you and do that for someone else. I have already determined in my heart that when my boys are older, I want to find some mother with young children at home and offer to babysit once in a while to give her a break. Why? Because I know what it would mean to me if someone did that for me (which, by the way, my mom just did for me the afternoon I am writing this. Thanks, Mom! What a blessing it was for me to get a break!).

I'm not saying to do things with the wrong motives or to fall into self-righteousness, thinking if we do good, then God has to bless us because we are just so good. God blesses us because of His amazing grace, not because we have earned it. But sowing and reaping is a spiritual law. Just like in farming, the harvest won't come unless the seed has first been planted. Galatians 6:9 says, "And let us not grow weary while doing good, for in due season we shall reap if we do not lose heart."

Hang in there. Keep planting seeds of love and blessings to others, and I believe it will be given back to you. When that thought comes of "I wish someone would do that for me," then take the opportunity to do it for someone else. Jesus did it all for us; if we will receive His love it will motivate us to show His love to others.

I honestly fought God a little bit about writing this article. I didn't want it to be written for any of the wrong reasons or for it to seem like I was hinting around for people to help me. I thought people might get the wrong impression. Also, I love for Jesus to be the focal point of my articles, and this one didn't mention Him much. But God just kept putting it in my heart and bringing me back to those thoughts: "Whatever you want someone to do for you, you do it for someone else." So finally I consented to do it and prayed that by doing so, someone would be encouraged.

Stacie shared my article on Facebook and commented, "What a fabulous article." That surprised me because I didn't think it was one of my better ones but believe that since God wanted me to write it He had someone specific in mind that needed to hear it.

Easter
The Almost-Too-Good-to-Be-True Holiday

I would say, out of all the holidays, Easter is my favorite. The reason is because we celebrate the resurrection of our Savior. It is remembering that Jesus finished what He was sent here to accomplish.

Healing, deliverance, prosperity, and forgiveness of sins were all part of the atonement of our Lord Jesus. He paid for it all so we would have no lack. I want to focus particularly on His payment for our sins in this column.

If you would ask a typical Christian what Jesus did for us, they would say He died for our sins. That is the basic foundation of our Christian faith. But do we truly understand what that means? I sure didn't used to, and I think most believers don't comprehend the depth of what Jesus did for us all in regard to sin.

I believed that when I got saved, all my past sins were forgiven. But after my rebirth, all my sins were going to be held against me, and I needed to ask for forgiveness. I would lie in bed at night, reflecting on my day and thinking of all the ways I had sinned. Then I would start confessing them and asking God to forgive me for each one, and at the end, I would ask for forgiveness for the ones I didn't know I had committed. I was very sin-conscious. Once again, I was falling back under the old covenant mind-set.

The people of Israel were always conscious of their sins because they were under the conditional covenant of the law. Their sins were never completely wiped away, only temporarily covered by blood sacrifices. After a sacrifice, they might think, "Oh, good, my sins are forgiven," but then they were reminded that it was not permanent forgiveness. Sin was always on their minds.

We are not to have that mind-set anymore. Jesus paid for all our sins. Isaiah 53:6 says, "All we like sheep have gone astray; we have turned, every one, to his own way; and the Lord has laid on Him the iniquity of us all." Note, it does not say the iniquity just up until we get born again. It is the iniquity for all people for all eternity.

If you are struggling with this, let me ask you this question: is Jesus being sacrificed again each time we sin? No. He only did it once. That was why He cried out, "It is finished," and gave up His spirit because He had completed the task that His Father had sent Him here to accomplish (John 19:30). He is now seated next to His Father because He has successfully purged all our sins (Hebrews 1:3). He bore all the wrath for our sins and permanently put it away, once and for all. Because of Him, God is not imputing sin to us anymore because it has already been imputed (or charged) to His Son's account (Romans 4:8).

Hebrews 9:12–14 states, "Not with the blood of goats and calves, but with His own blood he entered the most holy place once for all, having obtained eternal redemption. For if the blood of bulls and goats and the ashes of a heifer, sprinkling the unclean, sanctifies for the purifying of the flesh, how much more shall the blood of Christ, who through the eternal Spirit offered Himself without spot to God, cleanse your conscience from dead works to serve the living God?"

If we are believers, our conscience is to be cleansed, not bogged down with all our sins. When we are sin-conscious, we aren't Jesus-conscious. We should be conscious of all our sins being forgiven through his blood. (And contrary to some people's thinking, knowing you are forgiven does not make you want to go out and sin).

I know the transformation that has taken place in me by learning these truths. Now, instead of focusing on myself and my shortcomings, I think of Jesus and how He paid it all for me. He already suffered for every sin that I deserve to be punished for on His innocent body. He didn't deserve such punishment, and I don't deserve such grace. It seems too good to be true. But praise God it is true. That is the good news of the new covenant!

During this Easter season, I pray for everyone to reflect on the incredible sacrifice Jesus made for us all. Since He paid for our sins, He doesn't want us to be sin-conscious anymore. Make it your point to be Jesus-conscious instead, and thank Him for taking our place on the cross when we did nothing to deserve it.

Understanding the immense sacrifice that Jesus made for us all has changed me tremendously. My mind-set has changed from always thinking about what I have to do to thinking about what Jesus has done for us. I pray believers everywhere get a deeper revelation of what this means. It is all about Jesus. He has overpaid the price for all of the sins of all people of all time. Thank You, my Savior!

Do Not settle for Less than God's Best

I want Christians everywhere to catch something. No, it's not a fish or a cold, but it is a greater vision of the life that God has called each of us to live. I mean, God has amazing plans for each of us, and He wants us to do amazing things. I don't see many Christians believing that, or else our lives would be radically different. We conform to the world. If the world tells us we can or can't do something, we submit to it. We live in the natural realm, instead of living in the supernatural realm. We need to enlarge our thinking first and believe in that before we can start seeing the supernatural taking place.

I am not saying anything to condemn anyone, and God is not condemning us if we aren't believing big. But I do want to light a fire in some hearts so we can live out the abundant, powerful life that Jesus purchased for us all to have.

Let me give you a few verses to prove that God wants us to believe for big things. Now this first verse is straight from the lips of Jesus. John 14:12 says, "Most assuredly, I say to you; he who believes in Me, the works that I do he will do also; and greater works than these he will do, because I go to My Father."

Okay, everyone, read that one over again. You may not believe that is actually in the Bible. This is what Jesus tells us we should be doing: the same works that He did and even greater than that. Jesus wouldn't have told us this if He hadn't given us the power to do it. What kind of works did Jesus do? Hmmm, let's see. He healed the sick, lame, mute, blind, raised the dead, cast out demons, and showed the love of God in truth without condemnation, just to name a few. He says we are not only to be doing these things but greater than that. How many people are believing to do the same works as Jesus, let alone greater things than that?

Ephesians 3:20 states, "Now to Him who is able to do exceedingly abundantly above all that we ask or think, according to the power that works in us." Once again, what a powerful verse proving how God wants us to believe for big things. I want you to take a moment and believe for something big, something that would just blow people away and glorify the name of Jesus. If people would ask you how you did it, you could only reply, "It's all God! God did this, not me. I only believed for it." Now as big as you can think, God can do exceedingly, abundantly more than that. Isn't that mind-boggling? It is according to His power at work within us. That power is in us if we have received Jesus as our Savior.

Here are a few more verses to get you to believe big:

> I can do all things through Christ who gives me strength. (Philippians 4:13)
>
> For with God nothing will be impossible. (Luke 1:37)
>
> The things which are impossible with men are possible with God. (Luke 18:27)

Look at all these things the Word of God tells us. Doesn't it make you tired of living a mediocre, "standard" Christian life? What is considered normal today should not be. The normal back in the day of the disciples should be our normal now. We are disciples of Jesus with the same power that God used to raise Jesus from the dead living inside of us (Ephesians 1:19–20). I want to encourage everyone to desire to receive everything Jesus died on the cross to give us. Get that spirit of fight within your heart and mind that says, "I will not settle for less than God's best for my life. I have decided that I am going to fight to receive everything that Jesus died to give me, and I will not let that enemy steal it from me!" And it will be a fight. It isn't a fight to get God to move, because He has already moved through His Son more than two thousand years ago. It will be a fight against the world that is telling you to the contrary.

To be continued.

It is a passion of mine to get fellow believers to start believing big. I see it all around me that so many just succumb to things the way nonbelievers do. We should be different! We shouldn't think the way the world thinks but think and believe the way God wants us to.

A reader named Edward wrote, "Amber, I'm so proud of you. Love the article. You've got me thinking much deeper. You have a gift, keep up the good work, and stay blessed.

Thank You, Lord! It is all about You, Jesus, and may this article impact others also so they start desiring to live out the abundant life that You died to give us all!

Will You believe the World or the Word?

When I first caught hold of the fact that God had great plans for my life (as He does for us all) and wanted me to believe big, my approach to life changed tremendously. I used to limit myself because I looked at my own resources in the natural instead of what Jesus could do through me in the supernatural. Trying new things intimidated me. I remember being scared to try waitressing as a summer job because I didn't think I would be good enough and people would be critical of me.

Now, I believe for big things. If I start to think, "Oh, I can't do that," I remind myself that it is not me doing it alone, and with God working through me, all things are possible.

My family recently moved to a house that my husband and I had our eyes on ever since we got married seven years ago. It was totally a work of God. Anyhow, we decided to sell our other house without a realtor because we felt it was the best thing for us. There is no way I would have tried that in years prior. But this time, I decided that with God, all things are possible, and I can do all things through Christ who gives me strength. I wasn't going to limit God by my small thinking like I had in the past.

We listed our house the first week of December, which I think is probably the worst possible time of year to sell a house. But I believed despite the circumstances that God was going to find the right buyer for us and would do so quickly. I needed a scripture to stand on, so I found Psalm 34:10, which says, "The young lions lack and suffer hunger, but those who seek the Lord shall not lack any good thing." I said, "Okay, God, Your Word says that those who seek You shall not lack any good thing. Selling our house is a good thing, so I am going to believe Your Word that we will not lack this and that we will sell our house. Thank Your, Lord."

People came against us, saying how bad a time of the year it was to sell and how hard it was to sell a house on your own. I got a letter from a realtor in a town thirty minutes away listing umpteen reasons why you should not sell your house on your own. (How she heard about our house for sale by an owner on a little street in Baltic I do not know.) After I read that letter, I condemned it, saying, "Lady, you might be right in the natural, but you don't realize that God is working this one out in the supernatural realm."

Isaiah 54:17 tells us that no weapon formed against us shall prosper, and every tongue that rises against us in judgment we shall condemn. So I did that. I wasn't going to let what I saw and what people said against us in the natural prevent the supernatural from happening.

It wasn't always easy. Things looked bleak at times. But I just kept going back to the Word and the promise I had from it. So on February 10, we closed on the sale of our old house. What a faithful God we serve! His Word does not return void. Start believing in that. Hold on to the Word no matter what others may say.

If the doctor says you have an incurable disease, know that they are just doing their job by what they can see in the natural. The Word says that "by your stripes we were healed," so believe that Jesus has already provided healing for your body, even if you can't see it. Speak to your mountain (Mark 11:23) about your God, and believe it by faith. Stand firm on what the Word says, not what the world says.

We walk by faith, not by sight (2 Corinthians 5:7). Believe that God is working behind the scenes in the supernatural realm. If your finances look bleak, know that the Word says that "My God shall supply all your needs," and hang onto that, even when you can't see the manifestation yet. Let's let the Word dominate us and not the world.

People will probably think you are weird. They may call you a fanatic. But the fear of man brings a snare (Proverbs 29:25). Don't let what others think and say about you keep you from living out the victorious life Jesus died to give us all. Believe His Word above everything else, and you will see greater manifestations of power being displayed in your life. Now doesn't that sound exciting? It sure does to me!

I am learning more and more how much power we have as believers and how the word of God is the absolute truth! We need to put faith in that. I think this is an area where most believers are very weak. I am not where I want to be yet, but praise God, I am not where I was. We need to let go of what everyone thinks and says about us. I know it isn't easy. I have been called a fanatic, and I know some people think I am weird. But I think they are weird to let the world and things they see dominate them!

As I mentioned, it wasn't always easy to believe that our house would be sold quickly. But I knew deep down it would be because of what the word of God said, and I knew that God would get the glory for it.

He Restores My Soul

The other day I saw an old picture of my family on my dad's side as they were gathered together at my grandma Lucy's house for Easter. I would say it was from around 1966 or 1967. At first, the picture made me smile, as warm memories of family members flooded my soul. But then I started looking at all the family members in that picture that weren't with us anymore, and my happiness turned to sadness.

Instead of focusing on where they are now, I focused on the fact that so many people that I loved and who loved me were no longer here on earth. These people were supportive of me and thought I was special, especially my dad. To him, I was always Daddy's little girl, and it made me sad that I didn't have that anymore. I thought about how different things are now than when I was a kid and how many people aren't in my life anymore that used to be. I became overwhelmed with grief.

I was in a funk for a couple of days because of what I was thinking about. Instead of thinking of Jesus and all that I have now, I was wallowing in self-pity about days gone by. I needed a restoration of my soul.

The service at church the following Sunday helped pull me out because it got my mind back on Jesus and the hope that is in Him. Getting our minds on Jesus is so important. Isaiah 26:3 tells us that He will keep us in perfect peace, he whose mind is stayed upon Him, because we trust in Him.

I think Psalm 23 has some key truths to restoring our souls as well. Verses 1–3a read, "The Lord is my Shepherd, I shall not want. He makes me to lie down in green pastures, He leads me beside the still waters, He restores my soul."

There is a lot packed into those verses. Notice that it says we shall not want because the Lord is our shepherd. The shepherd takes care of His sheep, just like God will take care of us. We need to trust in that, and I think that is why that verse is directly followed by "He makes me lie down in green pastures."

We recently moved and now we have some pasture fields. When meditating on that verse, I envision Jesus walking me back to our field and saying, "Now you lie down here and rest." This verse is symbolizing that we rest because Jesus is taking care of us. When we try to work things out, He can't, because we are holding the reins. We need to let go of those reins and rest so that He can go to work for us. Isn't that a beautiful picture?

I think it says He *makes* us lie down because so many of us won't; we try to control our own lives. But just like Mary rested at the feet of Jesus, He wants us to rest in Him as well. Resting while Jesus works on our behalf is much better than us trying to do things ourselves. He wants to take care of us and He wants us to allow Him to do this.

In the next part, "He leads me beside the still waters," I picture Jesus guiding me to a beautiful, serene little pond. He has me just sit there and relax by it. It is so still and peaceful. This reminds me of Psalm 46:10, which tells us to be still and know that He is God. This is so important in our fast-paced world. We need to be still and get all the distractions out of the way so we can meditate on our awesome, loving Savior. Being still is good for our souls. It brings our focus back to what is really important, and that is Jesus. When we are still, it is easier to hear God speak to us. Too many times, we are too busy to hear His gentle voice whispering to our spirit. Being still before the Lord has an incredible calming effect on me.

Maybe today you are feeling like I was. I want you to try to picture in your mind what I did and also Jesus speaking this to you: "Rest in Me, My child. Allow Me to go to work on your behalf. Let go of those reins and let Me have them. Get your mind off everything else, and be still and know that I am your God. You are my beloved child, and I will take care of you. I love you more than you will ever know."

Oh, how Jesus restores my soul!

I remember exactly when God spoke this article to me. I woke up around four o'clock in the morning and was having trouble going back to sleep. I started meditating on the first couple verses of Psalms 23, and God just started giving me revelation on it. I had never truly meditated on it before. I was really tired and wanted to go back to sleep, but instead, I laid there meditating on it until I realized I needed to get up and write about it. So at five o'clock, I went up to my office and wrote that article. It really seemed to minister to people.

My neighbor who recently lost his father told me he loved the article, and he felt the same way I had been feeling in the first part of it.

Another lady named Carol wrote, "Amber, this really ministered to me. I've been meditating on the 23rd Psalm for a few months. Reciting it to help me fall asleep. Thank you for the article."

I thought that was pretty special since I have been reciting it to fall asleep as well, and God gave me revelation through it to help others out. God pays attention to even the littlest of details because He loves us all so much!

A WORD OF TRUTH

Judy,

God is good! I hope you enjoy this!

Amber Miller

A Collection of 52 Inspiring Articles about
the Love, Grace, and Goodness of God

A WORD OF TRUTH

Amber Rice Miller

TATE PUBLISHING
AND ENTERPRISES, LLC

A Word of Truth
Copyright © 2015 by Amber Rice Miller. All rights reserved.

No part of this publication may be reproduced, stored in a retrieval system or transmitted in any way by any means, electronic, mechanical, photocopy, recording or otherwise without the prior permission of the author except as provided by USA copyright law.

Scripture taken from the *New King James Version*. Copyright © 1982 by Thomas Nelson, Inc. Used by permission. All rights reserved.

This book is designed to provide accurate and authoritative information with regard to the subject matter covered. This information is given with the understanding that neither the author nor Tate Publishing, LLC is engaged in rendering legal, professional advice. Since the details of your situation are fact dependent, you should additionally seek the services of a competent professional.

The opinions expressed by the author are not necessarily those of Tate Publishing, LLC.

Published by Tate Publishing & Enterprises, LLC
127 E. Trade Center Terrace | Mustang, Oklahoma 73064 USA
1.888.361.9473 | www.tatepublishing.com

Tate Publishing is committed to excellence in the publishing industry. The company reflects the philosophy established by the founders, based on Psalm 68:11,
"The Lord gave the word and great was the company of those who published it."

Book design copyright © 2015 by Tate Publishing, LLC. All rights reserved.
Cover design by Nino Carlo Suico
Interior design by Angelo Moralde

Published in the United States of America

ISBN: 978-1-68142-307-4
Religion / Christian Life / Inspirational
15.05.20

Breaking Free from the Bonds of Religion

The other day, the boys and I were at a local business, enjoying the free donuts they provided at their anniversary sale. A gentleman approached me, asking if I was Amber. After I confirmed that I was, he shared with me that he reads my articles and had gone through some of the same things I did. We didn't get much of a chance to talk as taking care of three young boys doesn't exactly lend itself to easy conversations with others. He went back and sat down, and I started thinking about our discussion. What was it that he went through? Did he suffer tragedy like I had? Had he been under religious bondage like I had? I wasn't sure, but what I did know was that it had affected him. I could see that in his eyes in just the brief moment we talked.

Thankfully, as we were getting ready to leave, I had a chance to talk to him again. He started sharing that he had been works oriented and had based his relationship with God on his performance, just like I had. He suffered from condemnation his whole life because, as I have stated before, our works can never be good enough. Then he said something that made me so happy I wanted to jump and shout for joy. He commented, "But I have learned that it is all about Jesus. It is all about what He has done for me, not what I do for Him."

Oh, a more truthful sentence has never been spoken! He was right on, and I was so thankful that he understood the truth, and the truth had set him free!

See, religion has it all backwards. Religion says you receive Jesus, and then you have to work to please God.

You have to live righteously, or you will not be accepted or blessed. That is mixing the old covenant of law with the new covenant of grace. It is like putting new wine (grace) into old wineskins (the law). Those two don't mix, and it is putting the burden back on us, in turn making light of the incredible sacrifice that Jesus made for us. When you think you have to do things for God, you've taken away from what Jesus has already done for us. *He* is our righteousness.

Let me reiterate what I have been saying all along and what this dear man has learned as well: It isn't what we do for Jesus. It is about what Jesus has done for us. We put faith in the One who has done for us what we were never able to do on our own. Our own good works can and never will be good enough. Don't receive Jesus as your ticket to heaven and then try to depend on your own goodness. That is a slap in the face to our Savior! Our faith in Jesus is what makes us righteous in the eyes of God, not our works. Although you may be able to brag and receive praise from man about all your "righteous" actions, you will not earn praise from God for it. You will earn praise from God by putting complete trust in His Son for righteousness instead of your own efforts.

Romans 4:2–5 says, "For if Abraham was justified by works, he has something to boast about, but not before God. For what does the Scripture say? 'Abraham believed God, and it was accounted to him for righteousness.' Now to him who works, the wages are not counted as grace but as debt. But to him who does not work but believes on Him who justifies the ungodly, his faith is accounted for righteousness."

I love those verses. It couldn't get any clearer than that. I encourage everyone to meditate on those scriptures. Stop trying to earn right standing with God, but believe and rely solely on the one who has done the work for you and has made you righteous in the sight of God!

When you realize that Jesus has done everything for you and you don't have to earn your righteousness, it will forever change you. Grace does that to a person. It will make you want to live a holy life, but now with the right motives. It is no longer to get right with God, but because you are right with God and have done nothing to deserve it. Your heart will overflow with thankfulness towards Jesus. I can verify this from my own life, and I can guarantee that precious soul that spoke to me would agree as well. Stop looking at yourself and what you have to do and start looking at the one who has done it all for you—Jesus!

I wrote this during a week that I wasn't sure what God wanted me to write about. I prayed and asked for revelation of what to write, and that man I had a conversation with kept coming to my mind. It made me think of how many people are still stuck in bondage, thinking they have to do good in order to have a right relationship with God. It is an awful way to live, and I want to help set people free from that bondage!

A reader named Larry wrote me and said, "Your last column was a home run! Keep writing, be bold and courageous, for the Lord is pleased with you. Amen!"

When We Pray, We Need to Believe that We Will Receive

One of the things I struggled with for a long time was being single. I dreamed about finding Mr. Right and having a family of my own. The Christian college I had attended really sparked that desire in me. I don't know the exact percentage, but it seems like about half the people coming out of that college found their future mate there. Many even get married while still in college.

As much as I had wanted that to be me, it wasn't, which I am so thankful for now. I graduated from college as one of the few among my group of friends who hadn't found their future spouse. It was wedding mania for everyone but me.

Boy, how I desired a husband. I didn't have the revelation of God's amazing love for me or how much He wanted to bless me, so I didn't have complete faith in the fact that He would bring someone to me.

Basically, I thought He was holding out on me.

Marriage turned into something I yearned for but didn't know if it would ever happen for me. In my mind at that time, God seemed to be harder on me than others, so I thought He might just withhold this gift from me as well because I must not deserve it.

While my dad was sick and I spent half my time with him in the hospital and the other half back home working, I thought about how nice it would be to have someone to help me through that hard time. I felt so alone and desired that special person to walk along beside me through it all.

Near the end of Dad's illness was when I starting learning that God was really for me, not against me. I sure didn't know what I know now, but it gave me a glimmer of hope. My mom shared with me that when we pray, we need to believe that we will receive from God. Then a prophesy God had spoken to me the year before resurfaced to my mind. I was struggling with a relationship, and God had told me so clearly in my spirit, "If you let him go, I will bring you someone much better." So a few days after my dad's death, I prayed and basically said, "Lord, I desire to be married. I believe that You want me to be married and that You have someone special out there for me. I am ready for him to come now. Thank You, Lord."

It was a prayer of faith, probably the first one I had ever really prayed. Sure, I had prayed before, but most of the time, it was begging God. I didn't know how much He wanted good things for me, so I didn't know if He would answer them or not. Basically, they were just "whatever will be, will be" prayers. That is a double-minded man (James 1:7–8), and that is not how we receive from God. Our faith doesn't move God, but it reaches out and receives what Jesus has already provided for us by grace. Romans 5:2 says that through Jesus, "we have access by faith into this grace in which we stand." This time I really believed I was going to receive.

My dad's death was June 7, 2006. My first date with Mike was July 2, 2006. We were engaged that October and married April 28, 2007. I was twenty-nine at that time. Since then, we have gone on to have three precious boys.

As I am writing this, tears are streaming down my face. I am so thankful for our amazing God and how much He has blessed me, and it is all because of His unmerited favor through the blood of His innocent Son!

My husband is better than I ever could have imagined. He is an incredible husband and an even more incredible dad. If you find any mistakes in this column, it's because Mike didn't proof this one for me. I knew he wouldn't have let me submit it because he doesn't like me talking about him. Sorry, honey, but this needs to be said.

God has great plans for all of us (Jeremiah 29:11). God wants us all to prosper and be in health (3 John 2). He wants us to all live the abundant life that Jesus bought for us on the cross (John 10:10). What are you lacking today? Pray a prayer of faith (1 John 4:14–15, Mark 11:23–24), and believe that God is going to answer it. Now thank Him for His goodness and faithfulness!

I wrote this article a few months before I submitted it to be printed. I didn't want Mike to get upset because when I was first added on as a columnist, he told me that he didn't want to be mentioned in them. Thankfully, when he read this one, he didn't get mad, but I am still not going to push my luck and write about him a lot. I just really felt this needed to be said and that it would hit home with many people, which it did.

A reader named Kari wrote, "Thanks for sharing. I needed that today."

Another reader named Nancy said, "Good article, Amber, and it shows how God answers prayers when we believe."

I want people to understand that God has already provided all we need by grace through the sacrifice of Jesus, and our part is not to get into a works frame of mind and try to earn it but freely receive by faith what has already been provided.

How to Effectively Share Your Faith with Others

If you are a Christian, would you like to be effective in sharing your faith with others? Let me tell you the secret of how to do this. It isn't really a secret, because it is in the Bible, but I doubt most people have ever paid attention to or understood this verse. Plus, it is in a book that is only one chapter long, a book that I so seldom refer to that I often mistakenly pronounce it like a choice cut of steak. The book is Philemon, and in verse 6, it reads, "That the sharing of your faith may become effective by the acknowledgment of every good thing which is in you in Christ Jesus."

Did you see that? Maybe you need to read it again. It tells us clearly how the sharing of our faith can become effective. By talking about how worthless we are? How we can never do anything right? How we are just sorry old sinners but God somehow puts up with us? No. It says our faith will become effective by acknowledging every good thing which is in us in Christ Jesus!

In Ephesians 4:22–24, it says: "And you put off, concerning your former conduct, the old man which grows corrupt according to the deceitful lusts, and be renewed in the spirit of your mind, and that you put on the new man which was created according to God, in true righteousness and holiness."

We need to put off in our minds that old person that we used to be before Jesus and put on the new man that we now are because of Jesus. Renewing our minds to who we are now is the determining factor in causing us to live right and allowing our faith to be effective. We shouldn't be looking at our faults but rather all that we are now as a child of God. It is okay to look back at who you were before Christ, but never allow yourself to stay there. Always remind yourself and meditate on who you now are because of Jesus. We are free from condemnation (Romans 8:1) and completely forgiven (Hebrews 8:12) and the righteousness of God through Christ Jesus (2 Corinthians 5:21). This is great news!

Faith will start to rise up and become contagious as you talk about all the wonderful qualities that are now in your spirit because of Jesus. This is exciting stuff, and you will want to share it with others. Satan, who is called "the accuser of the brethren," wants us to think and talk about how worthless we are because he knows that is not an effective way to reach people. He is scared of people catching hold of what Christ actually did for us because he knows how influential we will become as believers. We then attract people from his circle of darkness and bring them into the light.

Sadly, many people have fallen for his trap. They do the opposite of what the verse tells them to do. They walk around with this sorry attitude, always guilt-ridden and condemned, or else they think they are walking in pride. It's quite the contrary. When you have that type of attitude, what are you thinking about? Yourself. Your mind is on yourself. That is self-centeredness. But when you think about all these amazing qualities that are now in your born-again spirit, your focus should go to Jesus because you know it is nothing you have done but everything He has done for you.

I would not be doing what I am doing if I still thought God was condemning me and I had to try to earn my right standing with him. But since I know that I am no longer condemned, I am completely forgiven, and I am righteous because of Jesus, I can share that good news with others in an effective way. I can't tell you how many people have told me they like my columns and how uplifting they are. I am not saying that to brag; I am making a point that sharing the good qualities that are in us because of Jesus is an effective way to minister to others. When we start saying that we are the righteousness of God and forgiven, we will act that way.

Are you struggling with having an effective way to share your faith with others? I want to encourage you today to start meditating on the amazing qualities that you have as a follower of Jesus, and as you do, don't be surprised when others start wanting and receiving those amazing qualities as well.

This was a scripture I wanted to write on for a while but just didn't quite know how to put it together. Once again, the Holy Spirit directed me on how to write it. I am so thankful for Him helping me because I sure can't do this on my own. It is obvious when I try to write something on my own (I don't submit those). They are flat and lack power. So sometimes I have an idea and start an article (like I had this one) but don't follow through on it until I really know the Holy Spirit calls me to and gives me the revelation of what to write. He is our help, our comforter!

A reader named Fannie shared my article on Facebook and wrote, "I love Amber's sweet and loving way of using words. A good read!"

Thank You once again, Father, for using me. May others start looking at all the good they have in You and share that with others!

What Does "Fallen from Grace" Really Mean?

We've all probably heard the term "fallen from grace" before, and we've all probably said it referring to someone who has fallen into sin. But according to scripture, this is not correct. God's grace is always there when we sin because, after all, His grace was given to us while we were yet sinners. There is nothing we did to earn it or deserve it.

So what does "fallen from grace" actually mean? I will show you what God's word says about it. Galatians 5:4 says, "You have become estranged from Christ, you who attempt to be justified by the law; you have fallen from grace."

Did you see that? How do we fall from grace, from the unearned, undeserved favor of God? When we sin? No. We fall from grace when we reject this grace given to us through the blood of Jesus and go back to the law, or self-works, to try to justify ourselves. The whole context of the book of Galatians is about how we are no longer under the law because we now have Jesus as our righteousness. Jewish believers in Galatia received Jesus and then were tricked into thinking they had to follow laws and rules to please God. They fell from the grace that had been freely given through Jesus and were seeking to earn their own righteousness. There are many today who still do this, like I used to.

Romans 10:3–4 reads, "For they being ignorant of God's righteousness, and seeking to establish their own righteousness, have not submitted to the righteousness of

God. For Christ is the end of the law for righteousness to everyone who believes."

We cannot earn our righteousness through our good works. God's righteousness is freely given to us through faith in His Son Jesus, and that is the only way we can become righteous. When we start thinking we can somehow earn our right standing with God through our good works and following the law, we forfeit this grace that is freely given to us by Jesus, in turn, causing us to fall from grace.

Romans 8:8 says that "those who are in the flesh cannot please God." I've studied and meditated on this verse and the previous verses, and whenever flesh is mentioned in them, I don't believe it is talking about sin. Flesh the way it is used here means "self-works" or "trying to justify oneself according to the law." When you try to justify yourself, you are not pleasing to God because you are saying you don't need Jesus. I think God abhors self-righteousness because it takes His Son out of the equation.

By the way, who did Jesus rebuke in the scriptures? The Pharisees, because they thought they were good enough on their own by following the law and didn't need Jesus. Our debts were too deep for any of us to even scratch the surface of repaying them. Praise God that Jesus paid our debts for us and we can now trust in Him to be right with God!

I want everyone to realize that we do not fall from grace when we sin. It is just the opposite; we fall into grace when we sin. John 1:16 says, "And of His fullness we have all received, and grace for grace." God continually sends waves of grace after grace upon us, even right in the midst of our sin. Am I promoting sin? No, absolutely not. But I am promoting God's amazing love for us even when we do sin, as we all do. His grace will never leave us. That is undeserved favor that He lavishes upon us.

So now when we sin, His grace is there to pick us up and lead us back on the right path. Your sin can never be greater than God's grace. "Where sin abounded, grace abounded much more" (Romans 5:20).

Maybe you think that you have blown it. You think God has written you off, you've sinned one time too many, or the sin you committed was too great. I want you to know that's a lie. God is pouring out His grace toward you because He loves you so much. We all need to understand this and receive this amazing grace that has been given to us through Jesus. Remember, the sacrifice of Jesus was more than enough to pay for your sins. Won't you receive this amazing grace today?

I wasn't sure what I was going to write about that week so I just started reading from Galatians, and this verse came alive to me. It was so exciting! I had never heard anyone use this verse in the proper context; it was always when someone fell into sin. I was excited to be able to use this verse to set the record straight. Thank You, Father, that we can never fall from your grace!

A reader named David wrote, "You are right on target with a message that this area desperately needs. I read your article and blessed God that there is a voice raised in the public arena shouting out the truth of grace. Characteristic of our modern churches, religion has replaced spirituality, and more than ever, we need to hear the message that by grace we are saved and that not of ourselves."

Praise God for all the people who truly understand grace and for this dear man for writing me. I definitely feel a call to reach the people of Holmes County and the surrounding areas with the gospel of Jesus Christ because so many around here base their right standing with God on their actions. It is all about Jesus!

About the Author

This book is a collection of Amber's highly popular articles featured in *The Bargain Hunter*, a weekly newspaper published by Graphic Publications, Inc. in Millersburg, Ohio.

Amber has a passion for not only reaching the lost but also reaching Christians as well. She loves to tell others about Jesus and His sacrifice on the cross so they can begin to live the abundant life He died for all to have. She has a heart for proclaiming the goodness of God and His amazing grace.

Amber and her husband, Michael, have three young sons and live on their hobby farm in Baltic, Ohio, in the heart of Holmes County's Amish Country.